D1233462

INTRODUCING MORDECAI RICHLER'S
THE APPRENTICESHIP OF DUDDY KRAVITZ

Canadian Fiction Studies

Other volumes in preparation

Introducing

MORDECAI RICHLER'S

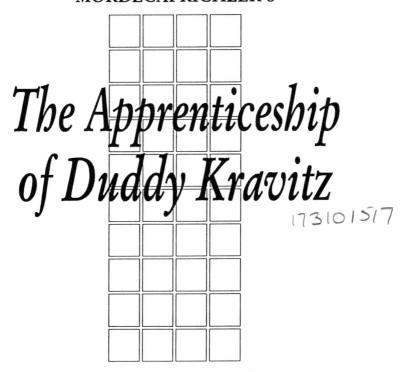

The Apprenticeship

of Duddy Kravitz

17310157

A READER'S GUIDE BY

George Woodcock

E C W   P R E S S

CANADIAN CATALOGUING IN PUBLICATION DATA

Woodcock, George, 1912–
Introducing Mordecai Richler's
The apprenticeship of Duddy Kravitz

(Canadian fiction studies ; no. 5)
Bibliography : p. 62.
Includes index.
ISBN 1–55022–019–5

1. Richler, Mordecai, 1931– .
The apprenticeship of Duddy Kravitz.
1. Title. 11. Series.

PS8535.I34A763 1990   C813'.54   C88-095237-7
PR9199.3.R53A763 1990

This book has been published with the assistance of grants
from The Canada Council, the Ontario Arts Council, and
the Government of Canada Department of Communications.

The cover features a reproduction of the dust-wrapper of the
first edition of *The Apprenticeship of Duddy Kravitz*, courtesy
of the Thomas Fisher Rare Book Library, University of Toronto.
Frontispiece photograph by Nigel Dickson,
courtesy Penguin Books Canada Limited.
Design and imaging by ECW Type & Art, Oakville, Ontario.
Printed by University of Toronto Press, North York, Ontario.

Distributed by Butterworths Canada Ltd.
75 Clegg Road, Markham, Ontario L6G 1A1

Published by ECW PRESS,
307 Coxwell Avenue, Toronto, Ontario M4L 3B5

Table of Contents

A Note on the Author

Born in Winnipeg in 1912, George Woodcock went to England in his infancy, and remained there until he returned in 1949 to Canada, on whose Pacific coast he has lived ever since. In the late 1930s he began to publish his poetry in magazines like *New Verse* and *Twentieth Century Verse* and moved into English literary circles where his friends included George Orwell, Kathleen Raine, Dylan Thomas, Herbert Read, and Julian Symons. He founded *Now*, a radical literary magazine which he ran from 1940 to 1947, acted for a period as joint editor of another journal, *Freedom*, and began to establish himself in the English literary world with his books of poetry and prose works like *William Godwin: A Biography* (1946) and *The Paradox of Oscar Wilde* (1950). Since returning to Canada he has travelled in Asia, the Americas, the South Pacific, and Europe, and has produced many travel books. Most recently he has been to northern China, where he travelled up the Silk Road and into the Gobi desert, describing his journey in *The Caves in the Desert* (1988). He has also published more verse; a number of important critical works including *The Crystal Spirit: A Study of George Orwell* (1966), *Dawn and the Darkest Hour: A Study of Aldous Huxley* (1972), and *Thomas Merton: Monk and Poet* (1978); and a number of historical works including *The British in the Far East* (1969), *Who Killed the British Empire: An Inquest* (1974), *The Social History of Canada* (1988), and *The Marvelous Century* (1988), an account of the 6th century B.C.

His writing on Canada has been considerable. He founded the critical journal *Canadian Literature*, has written a history of the Doukhobors and biographies of Gabriel Dumont and Amor de Cosmos; and critical studies of Hugh MacLennan, Mordecai Richler, Matt Cohen, Patrick Lane, and Charles Heavysege. Three volumes of his critical essays have been published: *Odysseus Ever Returning: Essays on Canadian Writers and Writings* (1970), *The World of Canadian Writing: Critiques and Recollections* (1980), and *Northern Spring: The Flowering of Canadian Literature* (1987). The first volume of his autobiography, *Letter to the Past*, appeared in 1982 and the second, *Beyond the Blue Mountain*, in 1987. He has won the Molson Prize of The Canada Council, the Governor-General's Award for non-fiction, the C.A.A. Award for Non-Fiction, the University of British Columbia Medal for Popular Biography (twice), and the National Magazines Award (three times).

Introducing
Mordecai Richler's
*The Apprenticeship
of Duddy Kravitz*

Chronology

1931	Mordecai Richler born in Montreal 27 January.
1940s	Attends Talmud Torah parochial school, which he leaves at age of 13, in 1944, for Baron Byng High School in Montreal.
1949	Rejected by McGill University for low high school grades, enrolls in Sir George Williams College.
1951	Drops out of Sir George Williams and goes to Europe, living in Spain and Paris until 1952.
1952	Returns to Canada and works as news editor for CBC.
1954	Moves to England. *The Acrobats* published.
1955	*Son of a Smaller Hero.*
1957	*A Choice of Enemies.*
1959	*The Apprenticeship of Duddy Kravitz.*
1959	Marries Florence Wood.
1961	Writes film script for *No Love for Johnnie.*
1963	*The Incomparable Atuk.*
1965	Writes film script for John Braine's *Life at the Top.*
1968	*Cocksure* and *Hunting Tigers under Glass.* Wins Governor-General's Award for these two books.
1968–69	Writer-in-residence at Sir George Williams University.
1969	*The Street.*
1970	Edits *Canadian Writing Today*, a Penguin anthology.
1971	*St. Urbain's Horseman*, for which he wins second Governor-General's Award.

1972	Returns from England to Canada for permanent residence and buys a house in Westmount. Publishes *Shovelling Trouble*.
1974	*The Apprenticeship of Duddy Kravitz* produced as a film with Richler's own script; wins Screenwriters Guild of America Award.
1975	*Notes on an Endangered Species.*
1975	*Jacob Two-Two Meets the Hooded Fang*, which wins the Ruth Schwarz Children's Book Award in 1976.
1976	Appointed to editorial board of Book-of-the-Month-Club.
1977	Writes film script for *Fun with Dick and Jane* and text for *Images of Spain*, a book of photographs by Peter Christopher.
1978	*The Great Comic Book Heroes and Other Essays.*
1980	*Joshua Then and Now.*
1984	*Home Sweet Home: My Canadian Album.*
1989	*Solomon Gursky Was Here.*

The Importance of the Work

The Apprenticeship of Duddy Kravitz, published when Mordecai Richler was twenty-eight, has long been regarded as one of the most important Canadian novels, one of the classics of a young literature. It is also the novel of which readers tend to think first when they mention Richler, the only Richler novel that has been successfully put on film, and the book that, though he wrote it less than half way through his life up to the present, most critics are inclined to see as his best, or at least as his most interesting.

Here Richler stands very much in the Canadian tradition, for among our writers what we are later inclined to regard as the key work, the quintessential book to which we constantly refer back in considering an individual's achievement, is often published early in his career. Sinclair Ross, for example, never wrote a better book, one that appealed more directly to our collective sense of ourselves, than *As for Me and My House*, which appeared when he was thirty-three. Despite a career of active writing that has extended into his eighties, we still think of Morley Callaghan mainly in terms of the novels he wrote in the 1930s — his own thirties — like *They Shall Inherit the Earth* and *More Joy in Heaven*. Though Hugh MacLennan actually wrote better novels later in his career, like *The Watch That Ends the Night*, it is *Barometer Rising*, published when he was thirty-four, that we immediately recall when his name is mentioned. Margaret Laurence's first Canadian novel, *The Stone Angel*, published when she was thirty-five, was that with which she caught the Canadian imagination, and many readers and critics still believe that Margaret Atwood's best novel was *Surfacing*, published when she was thirty-three.

It is a phenomenon one finds repeated in other nascent literatures, in situations where young writers must, so to speak, become their own classics: England in the Elizabethan era, full of brilliant young geniuses who often, like Marlowe and Sidney, died young with their life's work done; American literature coming of age in the Great War period with pre-middle-age writers like Hemingway and Faulkner, Eliot and Pound, producing the works by which they are most firmly established in literary history and, for that matter, in popular memory, works like *The Sun Also Rises* and *The Sound and the Fury*, like *The Waste Land* and the earlier *Cantos*.

1959, when *The Apprenticeship of Duddy Kravitz* appeared, was something of an *annus mirabilis* in Canadian fiction. In that year Hugh MacLennan published his best novel, *The Watch That Ends the Night*, Brian Moore published his first Canadian novel, *The Luck of Ginger Coffey*, and Sheila Watson brought out *The Double Hook*, which was the first genuine and important work of avant-garde experimental fiction to be written in this country. The stage was set for the vital decades of the 1960s and 1970s when novelists like Margaret Laurence and Margaret Atwood, Marian Engel and Leonard Cohen, and of course Richler himself, broadened and variegated the Canadian novel into a mature tradition.

The role of *The Apprenticeship of Duddy Kravitz* in this emergence of a distinctive Canadian tradition is very clear. It lies in the broadening and deepening of the scope of the novel, of what it can speak about, rather than in any real revolution in form. In many ways, as we shall see, *The Apprenticeship* was rather a conservative piece of writing, but it played an important role in colloquializing dialogue and in legitimizing that extensive use of the exaggerated, the grotesque, and the outrageous which eventually would become known as Black Humour and which finds its way into some surprising corners in Canadian literature, including the later fiction of Robertson Davies, which owes much more to Richler's pioneering in the exploitation of the absurd than Davies would probably be inclined to admit.

If *The Apprenticeship of Duddy Kravitz* thus stands at an important transitional point in the development of a distinctive tradition of Canadian fiction, it has a special place in Richler's own literary career. It was his fourth novel, but it was the first to gain him widespread attention and, in particular, to attract interest in Canada, where his earlier works, all published in England, were largely ignored. He wrote four novels after *The Apprenticeship*, at increasingly long intervals, with nine years between *St. Urbain's Horseman* (1971) and *Joshua Then and Now* (1980), and nine years before *Solomon Gursky Was Here* appeared (1989). Clearly Richler is a writer to whom energy and inspiration came early and have declined in middle age into creative trickles whose sluggishness is reflected in the tired style and the self-parodying plot of *Joshua Then and Now*.

One can in fact see Richler's novels in terms of a graph of achievement that begins rather low with the derivative Hemingwayish *The Acrobats* (1954), rises through the largely autobiographical *Son of a Smaller Hero* (1955), a second novel in the manner of a first novel, and through that troubled study in rotting idealism, *A Choice of Enemies* (1957) to the peak of *Duddy Kravitz*. Then it declined through the sinister clowning of *The Incomparable Atuk* (1963) and *Cocksure* (1968), to rise to a second, somewhat lower peak with *St. Urbain's Horseman*, in which Richler achieves an unusual combination of romance and dark humour, and then slide down the glacier to *Joshua Then and Now*, a much more technically accomplished book than his first novel, *The Acrobats*, but a less interesting one because its ambitions are diminished.

The diminishing of ambition is in fact what strikes one most on looking at Mordecai Richler's literary career, and this development has a particular relation to *The Apprenticeship of Duddy Kravitz* which in every respect — plot and characterization and theme — is a work permeated by the spirit of ambition. From novel to novel in his earlier period one sees Richler's ambition moving forward as he builds his energy and sheds his flaws. In an important essay on Richler, Kerry McSweeney has shown how these earlier novels differ from and even contrast with the later ones.

While the first four — *The Acrobats* through to *The Apprenticeship of Duddy Kravitz* — were technically crude and (with the exception of the last) heavily serious, they did have energy, passion, and a raw sincerity rooted in a dark vision of human possibility. The four later novels — *The Incomparable Atuk* to *Joshua Then and Now* — were much more technically proficient, but either had less energy and passion or had these qualities less consistently present.

In terms of the loss of originality and vigour in his writing, Richler is almost the classic example of the writer spoilt by success; sureness of technique tended to diminish the very rawness that distinguished his individual voice and that was at its height in *The Apprenticeship of Duddy Kravitz*, where it was united with that special sense of the absurd which the American critic Leslie Fiedler has defined as "a lust for surreal exaggeration and the grotesque, and an affinity for the atrocious — the dirty jokes turned somehow horrific, the scene of terror altered somehow into absurdity . . ." (Sheps 103). In the later novels the rawness of the voice is softened, for a new Mordecai Richler, man-of-letters and visiting professor, is now taking over, though the absurdities, now rather self-conscious, continue. In *The Apprenticeship of Duddy Kravitz* the raucous vigour of the voice and the atrocious absurdity of the action superbly balance each other.

Thus, *The Apprenticeship of Duddy Kravitz* is important for at least two reasons. It represents the early peaking of Richler's ability as a writer, and, for reasons we shall show in more detail later on, it offers the best combination of his special talents. Secondly, it marks the point when he was most influential in the Canadian literary tradition by producing a novel that helped to bring an end to that subjection to outdated conventions of taste which had held Canadian writing for too long in colonial stagnation. If the fiction of our country developed so richly during the 1960s and 1970s, it was largely because on the very eve of those decades two works so unconventional as *The Apprenticeship of Duddy Kravitz* (for its content) and *The Double Hook* (for its form) were published and attracted attention in the same year.

Critical Reception

Criticism is not necessarily a matter of a scholar or a book reviewer looking at a writer's work from the outside. Though at times there has been a romantic tendency to regard the creator and the critic as natural enemies, the act of self-criticism in fact plays an important part in the process of creation.

Many writers recognize this fact, and move freely between creation and criticism, of their own work and of that of others. Thus some of the greatest poets have been among the greatest critics, like John Dryden and Samuel Taylor Coleridge, like Matthew Arnold and T.S. Eliot, and very often such creator-critics have, like Henry James, written very illuminatingly on their own art.

In Canada we have had many examples of both the creator as critic of others, and the creator as self-critic, revealing the rationale of his or her own creativity. A.J.M. Smith and D.G. Jones, two of our best poets, distinguished themselves in charting out the ways in which a true tradition of Canadian poetry developed. Margaret Atwood has written with great illumination on the work of other individual poets, and, like A.J.M. Smith, has contributed the special criticism of choice which an anthologist has to offer; both of them edited Oxford books of Canadian verse. And some novelists have, in their various ways, written so illuminatingly on the art they themselves pursue that one is wise, before turning to the external critics, to consider what they have to say about their personal visions and their ways of rendering them into the art of fiction.

The approach of Robertson Davies has been mainly indirect, since he has argued out in the dialogue of novels like *A Mixture of Frailties*, and especially the later books of the Cornish trilogy, *What's Bred in the Bone* and *The Lyre of Orpheus*, all those burning questions of originality and faith to one's own time which the Romantic movement of the nineteenth century introduced into the vocabulary of modern criticism; in the process he has justified the conservatism of his own approach. Margaret Laurence has approached the matter of creation from a quite different angle. She has avoided making her fiction didactic enough for her characters — even the novelist Morag Gunn — to discuss the art of fiction directly. Instead she did so herself in a remarkable series of essays in which she raised the questions of time and voice that were so important to her.

But when we approach the critical view of Mordecai Richler's work in general, and especially of *The Apprenticeship of Duddy Kravitz*, we find not only a singular absence of any writing of his own that might be interpreted as literary self-criticism, but even a reticence in interviews, in which Richler is usually willing to speak openly about his life as a boy before he began writing and as a man after he did so, but tends to deal superficially with any questions regarding the structure of his works or the creative process through which he achieved them; he is notoriously reluctant to allow anyone to see his works in progress. Such reticence is in keeping with his peculiar record as a critic, both in his essays and in his novels, for while he has a great deal to say, in fiction and in articles and often very illuminatingly, about popular culture — sports and television and Jewish holiday resorts — he has up to now had very little to say about literature, including his own work, or about the arts in general.

One gets the impression of a natural writer who almost fears to inquire into the sources of his own creativity, and perhaps even wonders about their very existence. The alternative view is to consider Richler as the kind of craftsman who learns by practice — as he has undoubtedly done in his secondary occupation as film and television writer — and occasionally reaches a level above craftsmanship without really knowing why or how. This would accord with the remarkable lack of formal experimentation even in a novel as daring in terms of content as *The Apprenticeship of Duddy Kravitz*. In the later novels Richler plays a little with memory, but his handling of time is generally conventional and so, allowing for the almost obligatory obscenity, is his use of the language.

Thus, unlike some other Canadian writers, Richler declines to offer the kind of analysis of his own work that might be a guide to his motives or his self-critical methods. He will sometimes talk about the ideas that occur in his books, the issues they reflect, but about the ways in which such didactic matters are transformed into fiction he has almost nothing to say, and the critics have been left to form, with little help from him, their own conceptions of his work, which he rarely seems to welcome.

Richler's first four novels were all originally published in England, and only some years later did they appear in Canada, where the initial attention they aroused was slight. In 1956 Richler told Nathan Cohen that only about 200 copies of *The Acrobats* had been sold in Canada; because of the interest aroused in Montreal, where its descriptions of life and people on St. Urbain Street aroused anger in the local Jewish community, *Son of a Smaller Hero* was a rather better seller, but even its hardcover sales in Canada amounted to no more than 800 copies. Most of the perceptive reviews of these early books appeared in English and American periodicals, such as *The Spectator* and the *Times Literary Supplement* in London and the *New York Times Book Review* and *Saturday Review* in New York; the only significant Canadian notices appeared in university periodicals.

The Apprenticeship of Duddy Kravitz, clearly a book of greater maturity and originality than its predecessors, aroused much broader interest, though many of the reviewers, some of them established novelists, found the novel distasteful and, like Constance Beresford-Howe in *The Montrealer*, accused it of uncouthness and triteness.

Yet at the same time the first extensive critical studies of Richler's works began to appear. Warren Tallman, who reviewed the novel in *Canadian Literature* at the time of its appearance, later included a considerable account of it in a long essay on typical Canadian novels entitled "Wolf in the Snow." Tallman, an American who had moved to Canada where he promoted Black Mountain ideas about poetry, clearly recognized the American influences Richler himself has admitted. While D.J. Dooley, writing in the *Dalhousie Review*, found Duddy "utterly without decency" (qtd. in McSweeney 139), and dismissed the novel on moral as much as stylistic grounds, Tallman clearly admired Duddy for seeing "people for what they are, himself included," and for being "exuberantly acquisitive" in an acquisitive world. For this reason he mistakenly saw *The Apprenticeship of Duddy Kravitz* as part of a lineage stemming from Mark Twain.

From the weave of this erratic shuttling, a self struggles into presence, a naïve yet shrewd latter-day Huck Finn, floating on a battered money raft down a sleazy neon river through a drift of lives, wanting to light out for somewhere, wanting somewhere to light out for. (Sheps 80)

Two of the other serious assessments of *The Apprenticeship of Duddy Kravitz* during the 1960s were published in *Canadian Literature*. One, in 1964, was by Naïm Kattan, who rated the book as "its author's most accomplished work," and found its faults in Richler's apparent inability to go beyond himself.

Stirred by a demanding passion, he is led to destroy his characters through caricature. Facing a society which he wishes to conquer, he has no time to look at it, to understand it, to perceive its complete ambiguity. His characters are linear, for complexity would deprive them of the artificial consistency which is fabricated by a novelist whose wish to do battle is stronger than his desire to comprehend. This world without love or tenderness is at once sentimental and false — false because sentimental.

Richler manipulates situations and characters to fill a void which no degree of inventiveness can conceal. He does not succeed in breaking the yoke in which his sensibility imprisons him, for he takes no account of the sensibilities of others, and especially of his characters. These are his banner-bearers, the extensions of his own tastes and whims. (Sheps 97)

In 1966, looking back at a greater distance on *The Apprenticeship*, W.H. New noted in *Canadian Literature* that Richler's novel and Hugh MacLennan's *The Watch That Ends the Night* appeared in the same year, and used this fact as the text for an essay seeing both books as voyages of discovery into new mental worlds. In comparing them, he described *The Apprenticeship* as "a pungently ironic comedy" relying on a "sprawling picaresque method" in which the author always seems ready to "sacrifice the overall balance of his novel for the sake of big comic set scenes" (Sheps 69). Yet he finds a convincing self-consistency in the character of Duddy. We may not like him, he suggests, but we accept him.

The world of Duddy Kravitz is whole, and Duddy himself, while not particularly likeable, is very much alive. He wins readers to his side, moreover, because his reaction to traditions is a positive one. The control he wants, the mastery to which he is apprenticed, is a valid aim. His iconoclasm is of value not for itself, but because it is a route towards inhabiting a new world and fulfilling a social individuality. (Sheps 77)

In New's view, which I do not entirely share, *The Apprenticeship of Duddy Kravitz* "ends in a comic triumph."

In 1969, ten years after it first appeared, *The Apprenticeship of Duddy Kravitz* was published in the New Canadian Library with a rather pedestrian introduction by A.R. Bevan. Bevan distinguished *The Apprenticeship* from the romantic, individualist novel of youthful rebellion like *Sons and Lovers* or *Portrait of the Artist as a Young Man* by relating the hero to mid-twentieth century literary conventions.

He is a modern "anti-hero" (something like the protagonist in Anthony Burgess's *A Clockwork Orange*) who lives in a largely deterministic world, a world where decisions are not decisions and where choice is not really choice. (Sheps 85)

He also pointed out the central irony of the novel; that all Duddy does to achieve his ambition should proceed from his pious and reputedly wise old grandfather's remark that "A man without land is a nobody."

It is this last speech that directs Duddy's actions throughout the novel. Ironically, it is the comment of Simcha Kravitz, the chief representative in the novel of the old lost world of solid virtues and sound values, that turns his grandson into a person possessed of a materialistic demon. Duddy becomes a ruthless entrepreneur with an impressive list of sins of omission and commission to his discredit, and all to follow the dream implanted in him by the kindly old Simcha. (Sheps 86)

Bevan concludes that *The Apprenticeship* "comes to life through its dialogue, and the vitality of dialogue is usually a reliable test of the success of a novel" (Sheps 91). He considers that the success Richler has in fact gained is much more than merely local.

Written by a Canadian and about Canadians in Canada's largest city, this novel with its satiric-tragic-comic attitude to man in the modern world is much more than a "mere" Canadian work. Richler's novel, it seems to me, can stand on its own by any standard. (Sheps 91)

By the 1970s, Richler's work was beginning to find its place in those scholarly works that perform a double function of informing and enshrining. When the first edition of the *Literary History of Canada* appeared in 1965, Hugo McPherson's essay on "Fiction: 1940–1960" contained a longish passage on Richler's first four novels. In *The Apprenticeship* McPherson sees Richler facing a new problem, "the relation between realism and comedy or farce":

. . . though the exuberant reality of Duddy himself is never in doubt, the modulation of other characters from pathos to farce makes the reader's suspension of disbelief something less than willing. (714)

McPherson concludes by pointing to the ambiguity of the novel's ending.

Richler does not pose a final question, but one hangs in the air: Will Duddy reproduce on his own land the nightmare which he has escaped? (715)

The decade after the appearance of *The Apprenticeship* was a time when series of small monographs on Canadian writers were being issued by various publishers for the benefit of the growing numbers of students attending Canadian literature classes in universities and colleges. In 1970 I wrote a small book, *Mordecai Richler*, in Mc-Clelland and Stewart's Canadian Writers series, and devoted a chapter to *The Apprenticeship of Duddy Kravitz*. I also wrote the essay on Richler for the British volume, *Contemporary Novelists*, edited by James Vinson, in 1976. Since the leading insights and ideas of these two pieces will find expression in the body of the present book, there is no need for me to summarize them at this point.

Perhaps the most important of the more recent critical studies of Richler and of *The Apprenticeship* are John Moss's concise analysis of the book in *A Reader's Guide to the Canadian Novel* (1981), Russell Brown's piece on him in *The Oxford Companion to Canadian Literature* (1983), and Kerry McSweeney's extensive essay in *Canadian Writers and Their Works* (1985).

Moss, who had already made extensive references to Richler's novels in his books of criticism, *Patterns of Isolation in English-Canadian Fiction* (1974) and *Sex and Violence in the Canadian Novel* (1977), wrote with reservations on *The Apprenticeship* which, unlike most other critics, he rates lower than either *Son of a Smaller Hero* and *St. Urbain's Horseman*, both of which he felt had more of the "quality of heart." Of the novel he says, in summation:

> As with the best of satire, it is a sternly moral book, nowhere more so than when it is most humorous. Richler toys with absurdity and the bizarre, which he later exploits in *The Incomparable Atuk* and *Cocksure*, but generally he keeps to his conventions of social realism. His prose style is slick and sure, never pretentious or forced. Symbolism is entirely integrated. The imagery is reserved, although surprisingly lyrical on occasion. Richler can evoke the urban scene with knowing sensitivity. The whole novel is convincing, without being believable. (*A Reader's Guide* 239)

Russell Brown, in a paragraph that is mostly plot summary, sees an "assured narrative skill and rigorous style" in *The Apprenticeship* which in his view were not evident in Richler's earlier novels, and, like other critics, he notes how open the ending of the novel really is:

> . . . at the end of the novel the reader senses that Duddy, despite his finding victory emptier than he had anticipated, is not without achievement, for he has contributed to the ghetto myths an example of escape and has made something happen in a world that is too often static. (705)

Kerry McSweeney takes *The Apprenticeship* into an area of comparison with other novels written in English which most other critics up to now have neglected. Justly he suggests that, because of the writer's lack of complete control of his skills, the novel does not "withstand comparison with, say, V.S. Naipaul's *A House for Mr.*

Biswas"; rather, he sees it as "different only in degree from works like Schulberg's *What Makes Sammy Run . . .*" (166). McSweeney grants that in this book "Richler's natural voice as a novelist, which is brisk and predominantly comic" has emerged, but he contends that the novel is still "rough-hewn in style, technique, and characterization" (166). In summarizing his views, McSweeney declares his disagreement with much of the previous critical comment on *The Apprenticeship* which — he claims — "praises the novel for its mixture of slice-of-life realism (an authentically observed time and place) and serious moral concern" (168).

> But I would urge that the novel's moral pattern is rather too schematic and clear-cut, is hardly a challenging fictional subject — it is that of hundreds of North American novels and films — and is, in fact, one of the weaker features of a novel that might well have been a stronger performance had it been more thoroughly naturalistic in technique and eschewed the moral overlay. Had it been so, the major source of the strength of *Duddy Kravitz* would have been more readily identifiable: the raw drive of the central character, who is Richler's most forceful and memorable creation at least partly because he is an incarnation of the dark, negating energy of Richler's imagination. (168–69)

Here McSweeney is pointing to a fundamental dichotomy which runs like a rock fault through all of Richler's work: the division between an irrational, half-conscious nihilist drive that so often gains control of his imagination, and a conscious moralism that is intolerant of weakness in behaviour and deviousness in thought. In that dichotomy is embraced all of Richler's rabbinical background and ancestry and all of his rebellion against it, which seems so rational but in fact is the emotional and rebellious upsurging of a natural self, one of whose fictional personae is Duddy Kravitz.

Reading of the Text

LITERATURE FROM LITERATURE

The debate among critics as to how much literature owes to life and experience and how much it owes to other literature will probably never end. Aestheticist critics declare that the contribution of life, of what the writer has experienced and observed, is really accidental. The form into which he translates it, and which is what makes his work art rather than a mere reportage of life, is derived from other works within a self-contained cultural tradition. Wilde was only exaggerating this approach slightly when he remarked that "nature imitates art." What he meant was that art so conditions our perceptions that we cannot observe life without seeing it through the conventions of art or literature. And many modern critics, including our own Canadian pundit, Northrop Frye, have in their own way developed the aestheticist approach. It seems as though the ghost of Wilde were standing at his elbow when Frye declares:

> The forms of literature are autonomous: they exist within literature itself, and cannot be derived from any experience outside literature. (835)

And Frye goes on, in his famous "Conclusion" to the *Literary History of Canada* to declare that "Literature is conscious mythology," and that "In a fully mature literary tradition the writer enters into a structure of traditional stories and images" (836).

As a critic I have always felt that this is an attractively idealistic approach, almost Platonic in its pure extremity, but that — like anarchism in politics — it can only be sustained as a model of what should be. Ideally, all men should be able to live in free co-operation, but in fact no sensible philosophic anarchist believes that is possible in the world here and now, and so he settles for encouraging the tendencies towards freedom and mutual aid he sees around him. In the same way the sensible critic recognizes that the work of pure literature is very rare, and that while forms are inherited through the artistic tradition, content comes from life, and that there are always times when content will assert its influence in a major way, sometimes distorting the work so that it can no longer be accepted as literature, but sometimes creating a mutation in form that seems to be outside the tradition.

Nevertheless, the presence of an existing company of writers and of an existing body of literature when a new writer emerges will inevitably influence him profoundly, though it will be the accidents of life — where he happens to be and the people he falls in with when he starts to write — that will determine just in what way the great tradition will come to him and will help him to shape his work.

Richler was brought up in a household where literature was respected. His maternal grandfather, a well-known Hasidic zaddick, had written in Hebrew, and an uncle in the same line had been a popular Yiddish writer in New York, but when Mordecai began to write as a boy, at the age of fourteen, these were not the traditions he chose. Indeed, to begin with he seems to have been less concerned with actual writing than enamoured with the life of art, for at first he could not make up his mind whether to become a novelist or a painter, and the idea of becoming a career writer did not really crystallize until near the end of his period at Sir George Williams College. By the time he left for Europe at the age of nineteen in 1951 he had made up his mind to write, and to do it professionally in English, and from this time onwards, with minor money-earning interruptions, he lives by and for writing.

During his first period of two years in Europe, mainly on Ibiza and in Paris, the company Richler kept and the books he read tended to determine the way he would write. The writers he associated with then, and later during his residence in England, tended to be North Americans; he does not seem to have mixed easily with native writers either in Spain, France, or England, and his novels written in England show as little ability to empathize with English society as *The Acrobats* did to understand Spain, which he tended to see darkly and romantically as the home of lost causes. He once admitted that, while he admired the Angry Young Men who emerged to dominate English writing during the 1950s, and regarded Kingsley Amis in particular as a very good writer, he found virtually nothing to learn from them.

Indeed, perhaps the most striking fact about Richler's long residence in England was how completely North American he remained at the end of it. Contact with English life brought him none of the inner transformation and enrichment that it brought to other North Americans like Henry James and T.S. Eliot. English publishers and English journals were often hospitable and generous to him, but his general attitude to the English literary world was a mocking one that seemed to stem from a sense of insecurity, and on the one occasion when I encountered Richler in the company of a well-known English man-of-letters his attitude to the latter was embarrassingly and inexplicably hostile.

Yet in spite of Richler's rejection of modern English writers, the influence of an older tradition of English novel-writing is certainly evident in *The Apprenticeship of Duddy Kravitz*, which A.R. Bevan in his introduction to the New Canadian Library edition of the book aptly compared to Fielding's works, is very much a loose-jointed picaresque, a series of cumulative adventures in which a young man with no heritage and more vigour than principles finds his way in the world; Duddy himself stands quite firmly in the line of *picaron* figures that begins with Alain-René Lesage's very Duddy-like and anti-heroic Gil Blas and continues with the similar protagonists, half-rascally and half-innocent, who people the novels of Fielding, Smollett, and their imitators.

As early as 1956 Richler said to Nathan Cohen: "All my attitudes are Canadian; I'm a Canadian; there's nothing to be done about it" (Sheps 23). But he has also said, in his most recent book, *Home Sweet Home*: "Like many Canadians of my generation, I have only a fragmented sense of country. Home, in my case, is Montreal; the rest, geography" (70–71). And for the Montreal Jewish community in which he grew up New York has always been the metropolis, not London or Paris, so that to be Canadian, for him, has always meant to be within the American rather than the British tradition.

Given such a situation, it is not surprising that he seems to have been very little influenced by Canadian writers. Their realistic traditions, of the prairies and of the maritimes, have been rural ones and quite different from that of urban social realism to which Richler belongs. And their nationalistic concerns, exemplified in writers as varied as Hugh MacLennan, Margaret Laurence, and Margaret Atwood, have found no echo in his way of seeing Canada in a continentalist context. It is surely significant that the one Canadian writer for whom he has expressed unqualified admiration and who dearly influenced his narrative style, should have been Morley Callaghan, who also saw himself as part of the American tradition and, like the early Richler, was influenced considerably by Ernest Hemingway.

Talking to Nathan Cohen in 1956, Richler remarked that he had "more affinity with the young writers in New York, with Mailer and Algren and William Styron and Herbert Gold" (Sheps 23) than with young English writers of the 1950s, and this sense of closeness with his American contemporaries extended a preoccupation with writing south of the border that dated from the beginning of his literary career. In the very interview in which he declared himself a Canadian, he also said, without any apparent feeling of inconsistency, "I consider myself an American, and the modern novels I read were American. I read Dos Passos and Hemingway and Fitzgerald and Faulkner, and these are people who influenced me a great deal" (Sheps 34). In a brilliant essay on Richler's first novel, *The Acrobats*, George Bowering has shown how powerfully in that early book Richler was indebted to Hemingway, not only using the same kind of language and sentence structure, but also adopting Hemingway's peculiar romanticization of the Spanish people.

The American link was strengthened by the fact that most of the younger writers with whom Richler associated in Paris between 1951 and 1952 were Americans. Those of the group who have since made names for themselves included Allen Ginsberg, Terry Southern, Herbert Gold, and David Stacton. It was among these writers, associated with the magazine *New Story* rather than with the more sophisticatedly avant-garde *Paris Review*, that Richler first experienced the sense of belonging to a real literary world, which he had not felt in Montreal among the Canadian writers associated with *Northern Review*. Such experiences are vital in the life of writers, and often determine their later loyalties even in stylistic terms; Richler has continued to write with the colloquial dialogue and the unelaborate narrative forms he learnt from the Americans he read and those he knew personally. Indeed, among the younger writers he associated with one can find the range of attitudes that struggle for ascendancy in Richler's own novels, from a preoccupation with North American urban degeneration which Herbert Gold has exploited and which Richler uses in his portrayals of the Montreal Jewish community in *Son of a Smaller Hero* and *The Apprenticeship of Duddy Kravitz*, to the black humour, with its scatological and puerilely pornographic elements and its frequent excursions into parody, which Terry Southern made something of a speciality in his novels.

A further strain of influence was revealed in the Nathan Cohen interview when Cohen rather obtusely asked Richler if he was trying to "model himself on any writer in particular," forgetting that to accept the influence of a writer who can teach one something that will help one find one's creative self is quite a different matter from wanting to be a kind of literary clone of the same writer. Richler denied the intent of modelling himself on anyone, and went on to explain himself:

> Writers like Faulkner and Hemingway and Céline have understood this; and they have almost created their own vocabulary, their own approach to the language, so that when you look at a page by Faulkner or Hemingway or Céline . . . you know it is their book, whether it is good or bad. You look at a page, and you know that no one else could have written it. It is their window, and this is the state for a writer to reach. (Sheps 34–35)

The repeated references to Céline are important here, for they show another important area of influence on which Richler drew during those formative years in France. He did not form friendships with young French writers like those he formed with expatriate Americans, and there is little sign from his writing that he read with much sympathy the Nouvelle Vague writers who were beginning to move into prominence at this time. It was the preceding generation that interested him, writers like André Malraux and Céline who had established themselves in the 1930s and those — the so-called existentialists like Jean-Paul Sartre and Albert Camus — who became prominent immediately after World War II.

Through *L'Espoir*, his novel about the Spanish Civil War, Malraux was almost as great an influence on Richler's *The Acrobats* as Ernest Hemingway; the portraits of the communist Guillermo and the anarchist Luis owe a great deal to the revolutionary characters portrayed in Malraux's book. Richler's affinities with Sartre and

Camus can be seen in his inclination to put his characters into extreme situations where their qualities and commitments are tested, as Duddy's constantly are, and in his preoccupation with the antiheroic outsider who does not follow the overt mores of the society in which he operates. In this sense there is a great deal in common between Duddy Kravitz and the Stranger in Camus' novel of that title.

Richler's reference to Céline, which is a clear expression for admiration of him as one of the most well-realized writers of our time, is interesting for more than one reason. First of all, like Ezra Pound, Céline had made himself unacceptable to many people because of his rabidly anti-Semitic pamphlets issued during the 1940s. Richler's disinterested dedication to writing as an art was clearly demonstrated by his refusal to let his view of Céline as a magnificent original novelist to be affected by Céline's lapses of opinion. But it was more than a matter of tolerance, for Céline was a great satirical novelist and one of the darkest of all humorists, who deliberately created characters that were stupid, unpleasant, even contemptible, yet at the same time he involved his readers deeply in their tawdry adventures and strange misfortunes. Despite, or perhaps because of, their unpleasantness, the atrocious characters of *Voyage au Bout de la Nuit* and *Mort à Credit*, Céline's masterpieces, always seem larger than life. They are in the true sense anti-heroes, rather than non-heroes, because their negative forces are often as strong as the good forces that impel a positive hero, and so they stand as visible ancestors to Duddy Kravitz and many another Richler character.

LITERATURE FROM LIFE

Life contributes to the content of literature through the objective environment on which a writer grows up, and through the subjective reactions to his circumstances that help to shape him as an individual. Mordecai Richler himself has remarked that: "The first twenty years are the most important to a writer. After that, certain doors on experience close" (Woodcock, *Richler* 9). And, indeed, a reading of his fiction shows that the experiences most fruitful for him as a novelist were those of his youth in the Montreal Jewish environment from which he departed when he set off to Europe at the age of nineteen. The two novels that are concerned entirely with growing up in Jewish Montreal, *Son of a Smaller Hero* and *The Apprenticeship of Duddy Kravitz*, remain, whatever their comparative literary quality, the most convincing of his novels in terms of their portrayal of the life of a community; in comparison with the St. Urbain Street that comes to life as we read these novels the Valencia which Richler evokes in *The Acrobats* and the London which is the setting of *A Choice of Enemies* and *Cocksure*, are shadowy and unconvincing, lands visited in the mind but not inhabited as a native.

In so far as it is not gratuitous, fiction is a distillation of subjective experience rather than an objective reportage. But the way a writer evokes the setting in which he has lived does help us to understand the general character of his work and his perceptions. And the fact that Richler's perceptions of Montreal, and especially of its Jewish society and of the physical environment of St. Urbain Street, seem so authentic as well as being expressed in such an emotionally evocative way, not only indicates where his real roots as an artist lie but also suggest the kind of novelist he is.

In his most successful work Mordecai Richler is in fact a perceptibly autobiographical novelist, if by this one means a writer who wishes to remain close to the soil of his experience, of his personal past. This does not mean that either Noah Adler in *Son of a Smaller Hero* or Duddy Kravitz in *The Apprenticeship* is a literal self-portrait. Richler has always indeed preserved a kind of distance between the writer and the fictional persona by never resorting, except in non-fictional reportages, to first-person narration. Everything is seen and shown at a third-person remove.

Yet whenever Richler came to write of the scenes of his childhood, it has always been obvious that the writer and his leading characters shared with a great deal of intensity their perceptions of an environment they also shared. Richler even admitted that in a grudging kind of way in the "Author's Note" which he appended to the first edition of *Son of a Smaller Hero*:

Although all the streets described in this book are real streets, and the seasons, tempers and moods are those of Montreal as I remember them, all the characters portrayed are works of the imagination and all the situations they find themselves in are fictional. Any reader approaching this book in a search for "real people" is completely on the wrong track and, what's more, has misunderstood my whole purpose. *Son of a Smaller Hero* is a novel, not an autobiography. (xii)

So, on Richler's admission, we have in *Son of a Smaller Hero* the presentation of a real environment filtered through the subjective lenses of the author's memory and his perceptions. The physical setting and the special culture from which both the writer and his characters emerge are presented here with a great deal of faith and vividness, as they are also in *The Apprenticeship of Duddy Kravitz*.

I shall have more to say about this aspect of both novels in the next section, when I talk of *The Apprenticeship of Duddy Kravitz* as, in one of its aspects, a novel in the social realist tradition. But here we are concerned less with the faithfulness of the setting, of the social milieu evoked in the two novels, than with the real relationship between the central characters and the author, at least in his creative persona. It is, as I think we shall see when we look at the two novels as part of a disguised sequence, one of growing separation, through the process by which, in a mature novelist, the characters, always originating in the writer's mind, assume increasing autonomy.

Many of those who read at the time, in 1956, the disclaimer in *Son of a Smaller Hero* of any relation of the characters to people in real life, had the feeling that it was part of a defensive action provoked by Richler's justified fears that the novel would arouse indignation on St. Urbain Street, with its inhabitants seeking to identify themselves with the characters. For the novel is a typical *Bildungsroman*, the story of a young man's development through an individual rebellion that finally takes him away from the tribal setting of the family and the community to live his own life in the wider world. Even when they are not autobiographical in the sense of literally following the sequence of the author's life, such novels tend to project in fictional form the essence of his inner development. As Naïm Kattan remarked about *Son of a Smaller Hero*:

> Richler does not speak in the first person, but the autobiographical tone of the book is not entirely deceptive. It is the world of his own childhood that he reveals in fictional form. The adolescent hero deprived of childhood takes his revenge. (Sheps 94)

It was always rather obvious that, whatever else may have happened in *Son of a Smaller Hero*, the central story of Noah Adler gradually breaking his ties with the orthodox Jewish world paralleled the course of Richler's own liberation, as he broke away from the world of the Torah school and the synagogue, began to defy Jewish customs in his behaviour, and eventually made his separation definite by departing from Montreal and from Canada to make a life for himself as a writer in Europe.

How close much of the detailed structure of the novel was to Richler's life did not become evident until in his most recent volume of essays, *Home Sweet Home*, he included a frankly autobiographical essay entitled "My Father's Life," whose very publication seemed like a hint that we should not take too seriously, thirty years later, the disclaimer with which the novel appeared.

For what the essay showed was how greatly the leading Jewish characters of *Son of a Smaller Hero*, the three male generations of the Adlers, resembled their counterparts in the Richler family. Richler's father, except that he did not share his appalling death or his bizarre elevation into a ghetto hero, was remarkably like Wolf Adler. As much as Wolf, he was afraid of his father, the old immigrant who had prospered in his scrapyard, but, while admitting a younger son to partnership, still kept Richler's father as "a mere employee, working for a salary, which fed my mother's wrath" (62). Richler's father, again like Wolf, was afraid of his wife — and even of his son — and kept a diary "wherein he catalogued injuries and insults, betrayals, family quarrels, bad debts," all written "in a code of his own invention" (60). As for the parallel between Noah Adler and Mordecai Richler, it is revealed as being remarkably close, particularly in terms of grandson-grandfather relations. For Richler records how he too once caught his "fierce, hot-tempered" grandfather giving "short weight on his scrapyard scales to a drunken Irish peddlar. My grandfather, Jehovah's enforcer" (63).

Right in the middle of this curiously confessional essay by a man who often goes to great lengths to declare the originality of his writing and to defend the privacy of his creative activity, Richler reflects on father-son relations in a way that opens a sudden window on fictional processes.

Finally, there is a possibility I'd rather not ponder. Was he not sweet-natured at all, but a coward? Like me. Who would travel miles to avoid a quarrel. Who tends to remember slights —

recording them in my mind's eye — transmogrifying them — finally publishing them in a code more accessible than my father's. Making them the stuff of fiction. (66)

The stuff of fiction is indeed the endless series of perceptions and experiences that makes up our lives, transmogrified by memory and by the creative act. But it is in the transmogrification that the imaginative feat which is the making of a work of fiction takes place, and the more complete the transformation of the ordinary and usually meaningless minutiae of a life into an imaginative construct, the more successful the fiction.

The kind of progress one perceives from *Son of a Smaller Hero* to *The Apprenticeship of Duddy Kravitz* is an index of the degree of transmogrification, from life to literature, of which a writer is capable. Many writers never go any farther than Richler did in *Son of a Smaller Hero*, in which — apart from the remarkable portrait of his father *almost* from life — he also presents somewhat realistically the kind of problems, anxieties, and agonies a young writer goes through in the process of detaching him from his tribal milieu. Such novels are like initiation rites, or like the process by which an apprentice becomes a journeyman. Many writers, and some of them not the worst, remain at the journeyman stage because their talent fails them when they approach the master's task of assimilating what they have learnt, often painfully, of real life into an autonomous imaginative vision.

It was this step that Mordecai Richler took when he wrote *The Apprenticeship of Duddy Kravitz*. Here, more than anywhere in *Son of a Smaller Hero*, Richler gave substance to the remark with which he opened the earlier novel, that

The ghetto of Montreal has no real walls and no true dimensions. The walls are the habit of atavism and the dimensions are an illusion. (14)

It is not a matter of a lessening degree of realism in the description of the society and its setting between the two novels. Both of them offer a vividly perceived cross section of Montreal Jewish society, including its expansions outside the original ghetto core around St. Urbain Street. Indeed, as a realistic portrayal of that world, from childhood to old age, *The Apprenticeship* seems even more vivid and authentic than its predecessor. Here one feels, because of the documentary authenticity that underlies like a reportage the fantasy introduced by the presence of grotesque black humour figures like the Boy Wonder, Jerry Dingleman, is life portrayed as it is, yet shown to be an illusion at least in terms of the patterning the mind lays upon it.

In that added hint of illusion, that introduction of fantasy, *The Apprenticeship* comes to differ profoundly from *Son of a Smaller Hero*. Everything that goes into the earlier novel is eminently probable and plausible, even the strange communal hysteria building up around the funeral of Wolf Adler when the unfounded rumour is circulated that he died seeking to save the Torah. But Duddy Kravitz is intrinsically improbable, yet by the art of writing he is made entirely plausible, so that we surrender disbelief while we are reading of his actions; at the same time he is entirely *sui generis*. Nobody has ever suggested that this frenetic little entrepreneur is a mask for Mordecai Richler; nor has anybody found a model for him in the real St. Urbain's Street; yet in his own way he projects the untamed aspirations of thousands. Totally individual, entirely universal, as a character he represents the emergence of literature, shaking free its integuments of derivation, out of life. Duddy could not have existed without St. Urbain's Street to give him an origin and to harbour him as he developed; he emerged from the life of the street, his emergence is also metamorphosis, and if Duddy starts off in the world of the ordinary as a squalid and bloody-minded schoolboy, he soon changes into a being apart whose obsessive vitality shows literature outpacing the life in which it originates.

TIME PATTERNS AND SOCIAL REALITIES

Though fantasy tends to modify the action of *The Apprenticeship of Duddy Kravitz*, as Duddy's pursuit of land becomes more obsessive and leads him into a bizarre David-and-Goliath conflict (Duddy being a diminutive of David) with the grotesque Boy Wonder, it is in formal terms a very traditional novel. It opens up like a typical story of adolescent awakening with Fletcher's Field High School — based on the Baron Byng School to which Richler himself went in his St. Urbain Street childhood — and it ends before Duddy is out of his teens with the acquisition against all odds of the land that has been the object of his obsessive pursuit.

There is only one turning back of time in the actual progress of the narrative, when for a brief period we step out of Duddy's teens to the times when he was a little boy — seven or thereabouts — and the favored grandson of old Simcha, the cobbler with a sentimental passion for land who plants the seed of an obsession in Duddy's mind, so that in the end, following an old man's idealistic dream, he seems to become possessed by a materialistic demon.

Otherwise, the novel moves forward in a steady chronological progress, and this is appropriate to the action, for when time does eventually become a preoccupation with Duddy, it is because the present does not seem broad enough for him to make his future within it.

> Time became an obsession with him and he was soon trying to do two or even three things at once. He kept self-improvement books beside him in the car to glance at when he stopped for a red light. He did exercises while he listened to his records and in bed with Yvette he memorized stuff from *How To Increase Your Word Power.* (229)

Memory does not mean a great deal to Duddy; it is only the memory he does not have — that of his dead mother — that he hankers after, and that is stressed because it reveals a sense of rootlessness that drives Duddy forward with the desire to get his feet sunk in land, a desire whose association with his grandfather Simcha relates it to his family and the past whose clues might tell him what he really is. But, for the most part in *The Apprenticeship*, memory is the province of those for whom the present means failure, like Max the Hack, Duddy's ineffectual taxi-driver father.

There is of course another way in which memory plays a crucial part in the novel, though that has nothing to do with the chronological structure. It is the writer's memory, which provides the basic content of both of the Montreal novels. Critics have repeatedly observed the way in which Richler is always going back to his past. Leslie Fiedler regarded this as a defect, making *The Apprenticeship* "hopelessly retrospective" (Sheps 102), and Naïm Kattan remarked that "Whether he walks in England, France or Spain, he carries everywhere his little world, his secret fatherland, for he never succeeds in completing and going beyond his adolescence, which is its product" (Sheps 97). Richler admitted as much in an essay, "Why I Write," which he included in *Shovelling Trouble*, his 1972 volume of essays; he was — he declared — "forever rooted in Montreal's St. Urban Street. That was my time, my place, and I have elected myself to get it right" (19).

It is in the process of "getting it right" that Richler becomes what we would call a "social realist," which does not mean preparing a documentarily exact representation of the past so much as attaining a kind of imaginative faithfulness. We actually see a double process at work as we proceed from *Son of a Smaller Hero* to *The Apprenticeship*. On one hand the novelist is looking at the past more dispassionately, since Duddy's experiences do not come out of his own life as directly as Noah's do in the earlier novel. But the greater temporal distance from that world of adolescence had another effect. By the time *The Apprenticeship* was written Montreal had become for Richler less a matter of close experience. It — or at least the already vanishing ghetto of childhood — had been exposed for years to the Proustian reshaping of memory, and the outlines of experience while the characters had become transfixed by their own habits, their own fixed ideas, their own repetitious phrases (like "anatomy is the big killer" which all the Kravitzes use in telling of the problems faced by Duddy's medical student brother, Lennie). It is this rigidity of behaviour that gives so many of the inhabitants of the Montreal of *The Apprenticeship* the undeveloping nature of humours, and makes them into the appropriate material for satire and fantasy.

For the moment I am not so much concerned with satire as a major shaping factor in *The Apprenticeship* as with the way in which it both encourages and facilitates the social realism that is the novel's prevailing mode. For the portrait Richler offers of the Montreal Jewish community is a critical rather than a sentimentally favorable one; though he writes with the attachment of one who can never deny his origins, he also writes with the detachment of someone who has lived for years in other settings and cultures. This allowed him to become critical of the world in which he grew up in ways that gave him the reputation — among many who stayed behind in the community — of being not only an anti-Semite but — worst of all — a Jewish anti-Semite, though all he did was to portray the Jewish community as he saw it and not in accordance with its own treasured myths.

What he in fact offers is the picture of a class-based society whose members are moved by urges not very different from those of the *goyim*. The point he would have us always bear in mind is that his protagonists are not merely Jews — they are Jews brought up in a certain economic and social situation. In 1956 he told Nathan Cohen:

> One of the things I was most concerned with in *Son of a Smaller Hero* was that it seems to me that class loyalties in Montreal were much stronger than so-called Jewish loyalties or traditions; that the middle-class Jew has much more in common with the middle-class Gentile than he has with the Jew who works for him in his factory. (Sheps 32)

And later, talking of *The Apprenticeship of Duddy Kravitz*, he iterated a similar view of Montreal society and of his own work by describing the plot of *The Apprenticeship* as "the adventures of a teenage working-class Jewish kid on the make in Montreal, circa 1949" (Howe 123). In the novel itself the sense of a natural sympathy between the Jewish and the gentile middle class is balanced by a suggestion of an equal sympathy between the lower classes of both races: Duddy, for example, feels that

> with Yvette, he could be himself. She came from a poor family too and she knew that a guy's underwear got dirty sometimes and didn't look disgusted if you scratched your balls absently while you read *Life* on the living-room floor. (230)

The Jewish middle class hasten to remove themselves from contact with the working Jews of St. Urbain Street and the even poorer recent immigrants who live in yet meaner streets. Moving to suburban Outremont, they do their best to imitate the WASP snobs of Westmount, and even in the Laurentians there are all-Jewish resorts that fit in with the ascending pretensions of those who patronize them. Some are working class resorts on unpretentious ponds of murky water. Others reflect the prosperity of the manufacturers and merchants and sweatshop owners who visit them.

> Some sixty miles from Montreal, set high in the Laurentian hills on the shore of a splendid blue lake, Ste Agathe des Monts had been made the middle-class Jewish community's own resort

town many years ago. Here, as they prospered, the Jews came from Outremont to build summer cottages and hotels and children's camps. Here, as in the winter in Montreal, they lived largely with their neighbours. Friends and relatives bought plots of land and built their cottages and boat houses competitively, but side by side. (70–71)

It is at Ste. Agathe des Monts that Duddy receives his lessons in the class structure of Montreal Jewish society. He takes a summer job as a waiter at Rubin's resort. His fellow waiters are college boys on vacation; they mock him for his vulgarity and cheat him without compunction. The class war rages in the servants' dormitories.

Assimilation has entered even into the religion of the middle-class Jews. They have left the orthodox synagogues to the old and the poor and the conservative, and given themselves to a liberal Judaism in whose compromises Richler finds a mine of comedy as he shows Duddy, in one of his speculative ventures, making a film of a *bar mitzvah* with an itinerant English producer, Friar.

> The Cohen boy's *bar-mitzvah* was a big affair in a modern synagogue. The synagogue in fact was so modern that it was not called a synagogue any more. It was called a Temple. Duddy has never seen anything like it in his life. There was a choir and an organ and a parking lot next door. The men not only did not wear hats but they sat together with the women. All these things were forbidden by traditional Jewish law, but those who attended the Temple were so-called reform Jews and they had modernized the law to suit life in America. The Temple prayer services were conducted in English by Rabbi Harvey Goldstone, M.A., and Cantor 'Sonny' Brown. Aside from his weekly sermon, the marriage clinic, the Sunday school, and so on, the Rabbi, a most energetic man, was very active in the community at large. He was a fervent supporter of Jewish and Gentile Brotherhood, and a man who unfailingly offered his time to radio stations as a spokesman for the Jewish point of view on subjects that ranged from 'Does Israel Mean Divided Loyalties?' to 'The Jewish Attitude to Household Pets.' He also wrote articles for magazines and a weekly column of religious comfort for the *Tely*. There was a big demand for Rabbi Goldstone as a public speaker and he always made sure to send copies of his

speeches to all the newspapers and radio stations. . . .

At the *bar-mitzvah* Mr. Cohen had trouble with his father. The old rag peddler was, he feared, stumbling on the edge of senility. He still clung to his cold-water flat on St. Dominique Street and was a fierce follower of a Chassidic rabbi there. He had never been to the Temple before. Naturally he would not drive on the Sabbath and so that morning he had got up at six and walked more than five miles to make sure to be on time for the first prayers. As Mr. Friar stood by with his camera to get the three generations together Mr. Cohen and his son came down the outside steps to greet the old man. The old man stumbled. 'Where's the synagogue?' he asked.

'This is it, Paw. This is the Temple.'

The old man looked at the oak doors and the magnificent stained glass windows. It's a church,' he said, retreating. . . .

The elder Cohen had begun to weep again when the first chord had been struck on the organ and Mr. Cohen had had to take him outside. 'You lied to me,' he said to his son. 'It is a church.'

Duddy approached with a glass of water. 'You go inside,' he said to Mr. Cohen. Mr. Cohen hesitated. 'Go ahead,' Duddy said. 'I'll stay with him.'

'Thanks.'

Duddy spoke Yiddish to the old man. 'I'm Simcha Kravitz's grandson,' he said.

'Simcha's grandson and you come here?'

'Some circus, isn't it? Come,' he said, 'we'll go and sit in the sun for a bit.' (145-47)

The *bar mitzvah* scene is one of the big set pieces of *The Apprenticeship*, and the passage I have quoted conveys only a part of the load of incident and implication it carries. It shows very clearly the division in the Jewish community between the orthodox who wish to remain enclosed within their tradition and are usually poor people who have never got above the simple occupations of the early immigrants, and the second, more prosperous generation, whose inclination is to assimilate with the wealthy class of the city in which they live. With this end in mind they not only lay stress on harmony between Christians and Jews, but even adapt their religion and its liturgies, until old Cohen, with justification, complains that their worshipping places are not synagogues, but churches.

Duddy appears in one of his more sympathetic masks, handling the old man kindly, and in the process jeering at the pretenses of the reform-minded Jews. Yet we know that he himself is there to exploit the sacred *rite de passage* of his people to make a profit for himself and help him reach his goal of buying the land on which he had set his heart and which he intends to exploit as callously as any of the established money-makers among the guests would do, by turning the lake that strikes his imagination into another noisy, crowded, profitable, and landscape-destroying resort.

In this scene, as throughout the book, Richler is combining realism with satire, and taking it to the edge of fantasy. Throughout the novel realistic detail is in fact used constantly to give authenticity to the essentially unrealistic mock epic of Duddy's quest for land, which through its endless conquest of obstacles becomes as complex as any knightly quest for the Grail. Here, essentially, Richler is using an adaptation of the surrealist method, as practiced by painters like Salvador Dali in the 1930s and afterwards, which consisted of representing all objects with meticulous verisimilitude but placing them in astonishing relationships. Realism has always been a good servant of satire, as Swift and Orwell knew, and it adds conviction to fantasy if it is presented in the language of colloquial ordinariness, as Richler does.

THE APPRENTICESHIP TO CHARACTER

The core of novel writing, as distinct from other forms of fiction, like the fable or the romance, is the convincing evocation of character, a process in which the novelist's revelation of the person he is creating before our eyes goes hand in hand with the character's own development. A character is not created by the environment; he enters the novel with certain inclinations and tendencies which we see interacting with the world in which he finds himself. Whether his experiences destroy or exalt him, he leaves the novel more developed and more defined than he has been at the beginning. In the letter which he leaves for Duddy to read after his death, Uncle Benjy comes near to defining the process so far as this novel is concerned.

There's more to you than mere money-lust, Duddy, but I'm afraid for you. You're two people, that's why. The scheming little bastard I saw so easily and the fine, intelligent boy underneath that your grandfather, bless him, saw. But you're coming of age soon and you'll have to choose. A boy can be two, three, four potential people, but a man is only one. He murders the others. (280)

Essentially, the novel lives up to its title. It is an apprenticeship, in the form of a learning about the complexities of life and human relationships, that dominates the book as we observe the emergence from boyhood of that ruthless and yet pathetic being, Duddy Kravitz. The plot of the book exists to record and further the development of character, and even the didactic element that is strongly present in the book in so far as it is a commentary on Jewish attitudes, is always related to Duddy's quest and emerges out of his relationship with the people who inhabit his gradually opening world as he emerges from childhood.

"Where Duddy Kravitz sprung from," Richler tells us," "the boys grew up dirty and sad, spiky also, like grass beside the railroad tracks" (46). Cruel and lying and cocky, one might add, as boys so bred often are, and as Duddy certainly is. The novel opens in the dirty playground of Fletcher's Field School with the running guerilla battle which the Jewish boys of the school wage against the gentile teachers whom the Protestant School Board of Montreal impose upon them.

One master, McPherson, is an idealist ruined by the school system, who has taken to drink, and who clings pathetically to the single remaining vestige of his principles, that he never straps a boy. Duddy seizes on his weakness with the zest of a piranha, and virtually destroys him by making an abusive telephone call which causes the death of McPherson's wife, who rises from her sickbed to answer it. McPherson's bitter remark is one that echoes in the reader's mind though the whole novel. "You'll go far, Kravitz. You're going to go very far" (41). There are times when it seems as though McPherson's remark haunts Duddy like a challenge, and that the challenge is partly a response to guilt, for towards the end of the novel, when Duddy encounters once again his former schoolmate Hersh (a gentler boy who will eventually become the central figure of St. Urbain's Horseman), he returns compulsively to the incident.

'How was I to know that his wife would answer the phone?' he asked, his voice breaking. (263)

And he continues a moment later:

'If I had known that his wife was going to get out of bed to answer the phone,' Duddy said, 'I would never have _____ . . .' (263)

The other phrase that haunts and possesses Duddy is his pious grandfather Simcha's remark that "a man without land is a nobody." There is an ironic echo here from Richler's previous novel, *Son of a Smaller Hero*, when a Zionist agitator shouts: "The sheep have turned into dogs. Funny, isn't it? They want land" (27). As the story of one such dog-toothed, land-hungry sheep, *The Apprenticeship* can of course be seen as a satire on the Zionist belief that the acquisition of a land of their own will somehow solve the problems that history has heaped upon the Jewish people.

But Duddy's loyalties are closer and more primitive than those of Zionism, and even when he is obsessed with buying land, his first thought is to reserve a plot where his grandfather Simcha can settle down to cultivate the soil and grow better vegetables than the bitter radishes he rears in his Montreal back garden. Duddy is Simcha's favorite grandson, and when the boy was small they were constantly together, walking the streets of the ghetto.

But the round-shouldered men did not wonder or turn away when they saw Simcha walking with his grandson. The old man had no more enemies . . . . The round-shouldered old men looked at Duddy and decided he was mean, a crafty boy, and they hoped he would not hurt Simcha too hard. (49)

The theme of the small, loyal family runs through the novel:

'We're a small family,' Lennie said.
'But we stick together,' Max said. 'We're loyal.' (256)

Duddy's willingness to help members of his family at times of crisis is remarkable. When his brother Lennie gets into a scrape through performing an abortion on a Westmount rich bitch, and runs away to Toronto, it is Duddy who follows him and brings him home, and, in a rather improbable scene, persuades the girl's millionaire WASP father to protect Lennie from prosecution and from expulsion from the medical school. Later, when his Uncle Benjy, with whom he has never agreed, is dying of cancer, it is Duddy who goes to New York to fetch back Aunt Ida, Benjy's errant wife. Such acts of loyalty, and the occasional lapses into regret like his recurrent outbursts of guilt over McPherson, tend to mitigate the harsher aspects of Duddy's personality and make us feel more tolerantly towards him. George Bowering has remarked, in dealing with André in *The Acrobats*, that Richler has the "ability to take a basically negative character and to draw a sympathetic picture of him . . ." (Sheps 14).

Whatever their loyalties and their occasional generosities, Richler's "unsympathetic" characters suffer from an undeveloped power of empathy which tends to make them impervious to the needs and sorrows of anyone not tied to them by primitive biological ties. In *The Acrobats* we are told of Toni, who loves André, that

> . . . she felt fear, because she loved him with a hopeless beautiful love, knowing — always knowing — that he could not love, that something ugly and bitter within him would always stifle any love he felt for her. (as qtd. in Sheps 9)

And in *Son of a Smaller Hero* Miriam, Noah's Gentile mistress, senses even before the affair begins a ruthlessness in her future lover; her feeling is justified when he deserts her and recovers so quickly from any guilt he may have felt that, when he leaves not long afterwards for Europe, his feelings of regret are directed only towards members of his family; he has not a thought for her.

And similarly, while Duddy helps members of his family even when this seems to interfere with his obsessive pursuit of the money he needs to buy his land, he does not stop short of harming others outside his kinship who show love and affection for him and do their best to aid him in his quest for land. The prime victim of the latter part of the novel is the innocent Virgil, the epileptic poet and ancestor of the Flower Children of the 1960s, who becomes Duddy's devoted helper. Carelessly, Duddy allows Virgil to drive around as representative of the film distribution agency which is one of the projects he develops to earn money for his land purchases; Virgil has a fit, runs into a tree, and suffers injuries that will make him a cripple for life. But this does not prevent Duddy from hitting a low point of callous rascality when he worms out of Virgil the fact that he has received a legacy from his grandfather, and then forges a cheque on the sick man's account to make the payment on the last parcel of land he needs before the Boy Wonder gets his hands on it. The death of Mrs. McPherson through a telephone call at the beginning of the novel is echoed when Duddy and Yvette find Virgil lying unconscious beside his overturned wheelchair. "Above him the telephone receiver dangled loosely." The bank has telephoned Virgil to tell him of the forgery and he has had a fit. "Duddy ran, he ran, he ran" (309).

This final ruthless act not only alienates Yvette from Duddy. It ironically destroys the relationship Duddy values most. For when he takes his family out to exult with him over the land he has brought, old Simcha, his beloved *zeyda*, who had started him on his search for land, refuses to take the plot that is offered him because Yvette has already visited him and told him of Duddy's defrauding of Virgil.

> "I can see what you have planned for me, Duddel. You'll be good to me. You'd give me everything I wanted. And that would settle your conscience when you went out to swindle others." (315)

So, in the end, Duddy has his land, but at the cost of alienating the people who have loved him. His reaction is one of anger rather than defeat, for he now sees himself as a solitary fighter. "Nobody's ever interested in my side of the story. I'm all alone," he shouts after Simcha has confronted him with his deeds. A little later, coming back into the village from his lake, he sees Yvette, and she tells him she never wants to see him again.

> He gave her an anguished look, started to say something, held back, swallowed, shook his fist, and said, his voice filled with wrath, "I have to do everything alone. I can see that now. I can trust nobody."
> "We betrayed you, I suppose."
> "Yes. You did." (317)

The novel ends with a revealing scene in which the Kravitz family, except for Simcha who chooses to stay in the car outside, gathers in a village café for a meal. Max the Hack boasts to the strangers who are present about Duddy's feats, and Duddy, downhearted after his confrontations with Simcha and Yvette, is about to hit his father, when the waiter steps before him.

> "Mr. Kravitz?" he smiled shyly at Duddy, holding out the bill. "Are you the Mr. Kravitz who just bought all that land round Lac St Pierre?"
>> "Yeah. Em, I haven't any cash on me. Daddy, can you . . . ?"
>> "That's all right, sir. We'll mark it."
>> And suddenly Duddy did smile. He laughed. He grabbed Max, hugged him, and spun him around. "You see," he said, his voice filled with marvel. "You see." (319)

What we see — and what Duddy clearly sees — is that by the very fact of acquiring land he has achieved a metamorphosis. He has been raised by that one act from the class who pay cash and struggle hard to get it, to that of those who operate on credit. Like his Uncle Benjy he has made the leap from the realm of the workers to that of the proprietors.

What he will do with his success is not part of this novel, though in Richler's next novel, *St. Urbain's Horseman*, we meet him again, this time in Toronto, an unredeemed predator, once again running after an elusive fortune, and using others callously on the way.

Yet there is an odd naïveté to Duddy's reaction in the café that takes on meaning when we remember a remark of Jerry Dingleman, the Boy Wonder, when he decided to use Duddy to smuggle cocaine over the border from New York. "The boy is innocent. He's perfect" (138). At first this seems a strange thing to say about a knowing little schemer like Duddy. But innocence is not necessarily goodness. In its primal definition it is the lack of the knowledge of good and evil. It is, in terms of our relationship with other beings, amoralism. And there are so many occasions when Duddy is unable to understand the moral bearings of his actions, and sincerely views himself as the aggrieved man, that we must see him as an almost complete amoralist, a negatively innocent bring with only occasional lapses into moral awareness.

In Duddy's innocence — his amorality — there is much of *before* good and evil; he could turn out, as his Uncle Benjy suggests, either way. And this is what brings him into such a special relationship with the Boy Wonder, the St. Urbain's mobster whose immorality seems to place him — at least in his own opinion and that of his admirers, *beyond* good and evil. The Boy Wonder is a key figure in Richler's succession of dark presences, the grotesque and evil beings who are sometimes triumphant and sometimes vanquished in his novels; in this context I shall return to him later. But within *The Apprenticeship* he has a special importance not merely for the polarity of characters his presence establishes, but also for his changing role as Duddy's exemplar.

Max the Hack's tales about Jerry Dingleman and how he rose from flogging bus transfers to owning a chain of nightclubs as a front for less legitimate occupations combine with Simcha's declaration that a man without land is a nobody to fire Duddy's intent to become a somebody, and at first it seems to him that the best person to help him in his quest will be that undoubted somebody, the Boy Wonder, whom his boastful and ineffectual father claims to know intimately. The result is a progressive disillusionment and an ironic shift in the relationship. Duddy makes contact with Dingleman, realizing in the process that his father in fact hardly knows the racketeer, who uses the boy as a drug courier and later, when Duddy badly needs money to buy his land, refuses to help him. In the process Duddy realizes that the Boy Wonder is not in fact the widely known half-world figure he had first supposed, but merely a small-time local crook. The relationship develops into a rivalry, for Dingleman hears of Duddy's lake, and it is in haste to buy the land before him that Duddy forges Virgil's cheque. There is a final scene on the lake, when Duddy and his family are there and Dingleman appears, hobbling on his crutches and offering to buy into the project and provide capital for development. Duddy insultingly rejects his offer, and taunts the crippled crook.

" . . . FASTER, YOU BASTARD. RUN, DINGLEMAN. LET'S SEE YOU RUN
ON THOSE STICKS." (314)

Duddy has triumphed. He has snatched the land away from Dingleman and overcome his awe of the Boy Wonder. And yet, as the novel ends, we wonder if the two characters have not merged into a new Boy Wonder.

Richler once remarked that when he starts to write a novel he always begins by conceiving the people who will inhabit it and

45

creating the plot as he goes. As he told Nathan Cohen while he was writing *The Apprenticeship of Duddy Kravitz*:

> I know the people and the problems I want to write about, and I make up a story of some kind, which I very rarely stick to, and then I develop the story. (Sheps 41)

The result of this procedure tends to be that there are three kinds of character in a Richler novel, corresponding to three levels of importance. One or two major figures — Duddy and the Boy Wonder in *The Apprenticeship* — will embody the problems and will be thoroughly realized, dominating and motivating the action. A host of minor characters, often vividly and sharply rendered, will inhabit the background, give the local colour and act as a kind of chorus to the main drama. Max the Hack and the pathetic comedian Cuckoo Kaplan, Aunt Ida, and the rascally scrap merchant Cohen, are examples. They tend to be trapped, rather like the minor characters of Dickens, within eccentric patterns of action and speech, so that we remember the habitual behaviour rather than the person, which at worst makes such figures caricatures and at best makes them engaging humours rather than characters of any depth or complexity.

Finally, there are the people of middle importance, who often play vital instrumental roles in the novel, like Simcha and Uncle Benjy, like Yvette and Virgil. Despite their relative importance, these are the least memorable characters and the least well realized.

Simcha and Uncle Benjy stand at the opposite poles of belief within the novel, Simcha typifying the old generation of immigrant Jews who cling to the Chassidic traditions they brought with them from Poland, and Benjy the new generations of sceptics who have wholly abandoned the ways of the past, and who embrace the new ways with such enthusiastic confusion that Benjy wishes to become the replica of an English gentleman at the same time as he is a socialist radical well known enough to be denied entry to the United States. Throughout the novel the two men serve as embodied ideas, influencing Duddy by their words, but never developing into credible human beings.

Virgil hovers on the edge of caricature, and is most acceptable when we see him as a humour, a crocheteer dominated by his naïve campaigning for the rights of epileptics.

But Yvette, the personification in the novel of basic human decency, never really comes alive either as a character or a humour, partly because she is too good to be true in Richler's darkly conceived world of rogues and fools, but even more because he never gives her the speech that fits her background and never quite makes up his mind about where she belongs in the world of *The Apprenticeship*. At one point she is a French-Canadian maid in a Laurentian hotel with enough habitant shrewdness to help Duddy buy his land, and later on she is assumed to have the kind of skills and competencies that will enable her to take a job as a well-paid legal secretary. Even as a Québécoise she is unconvincing, for her English is not that of a working-class French-Canadian girl but of an anglophone member of the Montreal lower middle class in the 1950s. There is a strange kind of indifference in her portrayal, so that Yvette never lives in her own right or seems any more than the foil for Duddy's ambition, which in the end consumes everything else in the novel — and gives a final ironic dimension to the situation in which so many people are sacrificed and so many human relationships are destroyed for such a paltry end.

NARRATIVE AND DIALOGUE

When Mordecai Richler told Nathan Cohen in 1956 that the state for a writer to reach was one in which the reader could look at a page and know that nobody else could have written it, he was probably aware that in the novel he was then writing, *The Apprenticeship of Duddy Kravitz*, he was himself coming to the point of finding his own unique manner. His earlier novels, even up to *A Choice of Enemies*, were still rather laboured and self-conscious works in which, as George Bowering remarked when writing about *The Acrobats*, he had not yet "submerged the techniques of writing below the surface of the story as we are allowed a look at it" (Sheps 12).

What gives any novel its individuality is its special voice, and that is achieved by the critical balancing of narrative and dialogue. In Richler's case the combination that works in *The Apprenticeship of Duddy Kravitz* is that of a level — even flat-toned — narrative in an apparently conventional manner, that at times hits the rapids of absurd and incongruous situations, with a dialogue that is highly comic and carries forward the themes of the novel at the same time as it illuminates the characters who are involved.

47

Kerry McSweeney rather justly remarks that "at first glance" *The Apprenticeship* "looks like a naturalistic novel which dispassionately studies the determining influence of environment on character" (166). This is particularly so in the slow-moving early part of the book, the ten chapters that deal with Duddy's childhood and schooldays and offer the rather squalid history of the development of a conventional "bad boy" who is exceptional only in his unremitting mean-spiritedness. It is mainly the local colour, the comic sideglances at the Jewish community of Montreal, that hold one's attention until the beginning of chapter ii, part i, when the novel comes alive with the phrase, "Duddy found the land he wanted quite by accident" (67), and the action suddenly takes on pace and real conflict as Duddy emerges as a boy whose growth into adult individuality is marked by an obsessive passion that sets him off from his fellows.

As I and others have noted elsewhere, the shape the novel now assumes is a free-running and rather sprawling one, a picaresque form which is given shape by the counter-pattern of defeats that runs parallel to Duddy's stage-by-stage victory in winning his land.

The defeats begin early in the novel, when Duddy finds his father earning part of his living as a pimp, soliciting among his fares customers for a local prostitute. For a while he works in his Uncle Benjy's factory and tries to protect him against thieving *goy* workers, only to be dismissed as a sneak. His brother Lennie, going through an assimilationist phase, denounces him as a money-mad *pusherke*, one of the Jews on the make who create anti-Semitism. He establishes a bizarre relationship with the Westmount millionaire Calder, only to be disappointed when his request for a loan is treated by Calder as an offence to the spirit of their "friendship." Mr. Friar, the filmmaker with whom he works, absconds with the equipment Duddy has bought. The Outremont boys with whom he works as a waiter at Ste. Agathe persecute him and involve him in a rigged roulette game in which Duddy loses the first savings he has set aside for his land. His Uncle Benjy leaves him a large house but forbids him to sell or lease it so that he cannot use it to raise the money he needs. The Boy Wonder changes from an admired example into a despised rival. Virgil's successive misfortunes, for which Duddy is mainly responsible, haunt him. And at the end Simcha, his beloved *zeyda*, rejects him.

Somehow or other, like the hero of a conventional picaresque,

Duddy always comes out on top in the end, but often in ways that make the sense of defeat linger because we feel Duddy has discredited himself in the process of winning, and so the irony that pervades the novel is deepened constantly until the grand ironic question we have already observed hanging over its end. For though Duddy does not see it in this way, we as readers are likely to look on his victory over the Boy Wonder in rather the same way as King Pyrrhus of Epirus looked on his costly and famous victory over the Romans at Asculum: "One more such victory and we are lost." Duddy's sad situation in *St. Urbain's Horseman* suggests that his victory in *The Apprenticeship* was a true Pyrrhic one.

Apart from shifting the classic picaresque roller coaster of defeat and triumph into the ironic pattern where victory and defeat are barely distinguishable, Richler also accelerated the regular narration of the customary chronologically arranged realistic novel by introducing devices he had learnt from the occupation of writing film scripts to earn the money he needed to keep alive during his early years in England. The novel is full of quick cuts that hasten the pace, of closeup and angular shots, and particularly of setpiece scenes in which the combination of well-paced dialogue and visual flashes present the action with compelling immediacy. The best comic scenes in the novel, such as the graduation ceremony at Fletcher's Field School, the roulette game at Robin's resort, the bringing home of wandering Aunt Ida to dying Uncle Benjy, and, best of all, the screening of the film of Bernie Cohen's *bar mitzvah*, are constructed in this way; in the case of the *bar mitzvah* we are actually given a selection of the shooting script for the film, interspersed with the comments of the Cohens and their guests as they watch it and recognize each other on screen, and the juxtaposition results in very successful comedy.

All these devices, together with an almost imagist eye for the small, surprising detail that heightens the comic incongruity of people's behaviour, take the place of stylistic embellishment, and enable Richler to write a simple and even at times a rather level narrative prose. But it is the dialogue that in *The Apprenticeship of Duddy Kravitz* both reveals the characters and keeps the themes — or "problems" as Richler might prefer to call them — moving in our minds.

While the characters in early novels like *The Acrobats* and *Son of a Smaller Hero* tended to be introspective, often indulging in adolescently mawkish interior monologues, the characters in *The Apprenticeship* spend little time on reflection or rumination. They externalize almost everything into dialogue, which thus carries the burden of meaning and for this reason acquires a genuine dramatic quality.

Yet these are characters that in fact live very much within themselves, solitary among their individual thoughts and hopes and — in Duddy's case — calculations, and Richler is almost as good as Chekhov at creating the kind of cross purpose dialogue that depends on minds running apart even when bodies come together. An example is the scene in which Yvette, thinking of a good isolated place to picnic and make love, takes Duddy to the lake. But as soon as he sees the lake, with the empty fields around it, his lust turns from Yvette to fields and water. But he does not tell her immediately what is in his mind and so the conversation drifts into misunderstanding as she fails to comprehend what is so strangely exciting him and his mental calculations go on almost unaware of her presence. He asks her not to tell anybody they have been there, and she thinks it is because he is ashamed of having been with her. Then he offers her money to keep quiet, and she is offended.

"You wouldn't be ashamed if you had come here with Linda. You'd never offer her money, either."

"Oh, Yvette. Yvette. You don't understand. Let's go back and look at the lake again."

The lowering sun blazed behind the mountain. He's all skin and bones, she thought, and she picked up his shirt and trousers. "Take these," she said. "You mustn't catch a chill."

Duddy made love quickly to Yvette by the shore.

"I feel so good," she said. "Do you feel good?"

He could watch the lake over her shoulder and in his mind's eye it was not only already his but the children's camp and the hotel were already going up. On the far side there was a farm reserved for his grandfather.

"I've never felt better."

"Do you like me? A little, even."

"Sure. Sure thing."

He would have to buy up the surrounding fields with infinite care. Guile was required. Otherwise prices would surely sky-rocket overnight. Yvette lit a cigarette for him and Duddy decided where he would put the camp play field. The land there is as flat as a pool table, he thought. It's a natural. His heart began to pound again and he laughed more happily than he had ever laughed before.

"What's so funny?"

"Wha'?"

"You were laughing."

Once the land was his, and he would get it if it took him twenty years, he could raise money for construction by incorporating the project and selling shares. He would never surrender control, of course.

"Do you trust me, Yvette?"

"Yes."

"I want to buy this lake."

She didn't laugh.

"I'm going to build a children's camp and a hotel here. I want to make a town. Ste Agathe is getting very crowded and five years from now people will be looking for other places to go."

"That's true."

"A man without land is nobody," he said.

Yvette felt that his forehead was hot and she made a pillow for him out of a towel. (99–100)

Not only do the more sharply etched lesser characters like Mack the Hack, Cuckoo Kaplan, and Mr. Cohen have their distinct speech habits, full of verbal tics which proclaim their eccentric humours, but there is a perceptible class difference in patterns of speech. Richler's working class people may be able to create ingenious schemes for making money, but they have little in the way of active intellectual lives, and this means that they tend to think in clichés which are represented in their conversation by the pet phrases which have formed a pattern in one's mind by the time the book comes to an end: "That's show biz"; "Anatomy's the big killer"; "A man without land is nobody"; "We're a small family, but we're loyal." The phrases represent genuine attitudes, but they also reflect how their speakers have been imprisoned — even and perhaps especially Duddy — in narrow aims.

There are a few people whose conversation does represent a broader sweep of thought, and these — with the exception of Hersh who is a genuine and natural intellectual — are people with money and the leisure to pursue intellectual matters. But because they have no real imagination to go with their culture, this makes them ponderous in conversation, like Calder who treats Duddy as a kind of anthropological curiosity, or Uncle Benjy, that Quixotically noble man who pretends to be impotent so that nobody shall suspect his wife of being sterile, and whose death letter is ironically more profoundly alive than any of his conversation. Knowledge and leisure misapplied turn into comedy with Aunt Ida, who happily and drunkenly blabbers Freud to Duddy as he brings her home in the train from New York.

Nothing could surprise him by then, so that when after a few more drinks the conversation turned dirty he was not shocked. Aunt Ida confessed that if their horizontal relationship had been a failure then she was not blameless. There had been her own problem of penis envy, for instance, and this she illustrated with some smutty stories about her childhood. Uncle Benjy, she said, was an oral fetishist, and when she explained that for him he blushed and quickly ordered another drink. Then she turned her attention on Duddy and, hoping to distract her, he talked about Yvette.

"The Oedipus," Aunt Ida said.

"Wha'?"

"Your mother was taken from you when you were young and all your life you've been searching for a woman to replace her. All boys want to have sexual relations with their mothers," she said.

"Hey," Duddy said, "enough's enough."

"Don't tell me you're a prude?"

"My mother's been dead for years. I don't want her talked about like that."

"You see. I hit a vulnerable spot. That's why you lost your temper."

'Oh, for Christ's sake!" (240–41)

Because there is virtually no interior monologue in *The Apprenticeship of Duddy Kravitz*, and little more than the most elementary calculations are recorded in the way of thought, the characters are what they say as much as what they do, and it is in interpreting their dialogue, with a sharp eye for lies and evasions (which have their own significance) that we understand not only their actions but also their natures.

SATIRE AND FARCE

The essential dialectic of *The Apprenticeship of Duddy Kravitz* rests in the tension between the realist or even naturalist narrative, a rather static factor, and the strong element of satire, merging into farce, that provides the necessary moving force of the novel.

It is through the satire that the novel becomes didactic, for satire always involves the implicit statement of a moral position. The satirist measures what he sees by what he thinks should be, and strives by mockery to draw attention to and perhaps even correct the disparity.

Here we should consider the kind of writer Mordecai Richler actually is. He is not merely a novelist and short story writer. He has also done a great deal of pot-boiling work writing film and television scripts, and, more important, he has been an active journalist, writing articles and essays that up to now have been sufficient to fill six volumes. When one considers that he has written only eight novels, it is evident that this body of non-fictional writing forms an important part of his work. This is all the more so since, in his journalism as distinct from his film work, Richler has rarely written merely to earn money. He writes because he thinks he has something important to say about what he sees happening in the world around him, and in this he is in the tradition of the classic men-of-letters, who are willing to turn their hands to any genre and who live in many-facetted mental worlds where sharply defined barriers do not exist between a principal genre (in Richler's case fiction) and the lesser genres. With such writers ideas and situations move freely between fiction, essays, and more intimate forms of writing like journals, and their imaginative writing tends to retain the intellectual concentration which their other work demands. Writers like Huxley and Orwell and Koestler, like Camus and Sartre, fall into this category, and I think we can count Richler among them.

Thinking in terms of psychological types of writers, one can hardly consider Richler an intuitive novelist; he is indeed a rather clumsy hand at dealing with the feelings of his characters, as he showed when he plunged too deeply into the life of the emotions in *Joshua Then and Now*. At his best he is an essentially intellectual novelist, concerned with manners and ideas, and it is here that his fiction and his essays come together.

In the essays Richler is likely to attack directly the bogus and the pretentious wherever he sees it in modern life; his exposure of the hollowness of Canadian nationalism, his criticism of the uncritical approach by which Canadian literature cultists inflate the importance of essentially minor writers in order to have instant classics, his exposure of the hollowness of attempts by his fellow Jews to present themselves as a special people, detached from and in some way superior to the larger community, have earned him a good deal of hostility, which in his own curmudgeonly way he has seemed to welcome, so that the title of his third novel, *A Choice of Enemies*, finds an echo in his own life.

Richler's satire, in *The Apprenticeship of Duddy Kravitz*, as in his other novels, tends to be social and cultural rather than in any broad way political. Where it is political it tends to be concerned with issues that in Canadian terms are local, issues of the Montreal Jewish community such as Zionism and the lingering Communist echoes of the 1930s. Canadian politics in the broader sense is barely touched upon. One gains the impression of very local concerns and international concerns, but nothing between, as if Canada were an irrelevant no man's land between the microcosm of St. Urbain's Street and the macrocosm of the North American sub-continent and the world.

The objects of Richler's satire in *The Apprenticeship of Duddy Kravitz* are mainly the issues of which he himself became aware during his own childhood and adolescence (that crucially important first twenty years) on St. Urbain Street and in the community that centred there. Sometimes they were issues that moved him when he was young but which he quickly began to look on with a more critical eye.

One was Zionism. On one level Duddy is the quintessential Zionist, even though he is seeking land in the Laurentians rather than in Palestine. Just as Duddy and his *zeyda* believe that a man without land is a nobody, so the Zionists believe that Jews are only completely

Jews when they have a land — a patch of soil and water and trees — which they can call their home. To Richler, who believes that a Jew belongs where he is, like any other man, and who sees his loyalties as North American rather than Middle Eastern, the attempt of the Jews to see themselves as culturally separate from their neighbours is as futile as it is for Canadians to see themselves outside the general North American culture. His remark in *Son of a Smaller Hero* that the only walls to the ghetto of Montreal are "the habit of atavism" and that its "dimensions are an illusion" (14) clearly represents his attitude to the attempt by Zionists to abstract the Jews from the societies into which they have been grafted, as other immigrants are, by history. Just as the victory that comes to Duddy after his frantic efforts looks like a Pyrrhic one, so the victories of Zionism will always be equivocal and uncertain.

Richler is similarly critical of the attempts of liberal Jews to invent ways in which they can seem to retain their traditions while compromising with the non-Jewish world. Though he himself abandoned orthodox Judaism in his teens, he does not deal harshly with those who for reasons of their own keep to the old ways, and he treats gently people like Simcha who evidently gain some private mystical fulfillment from their Chassidic fundamentalism. It is only when genuine orthodox devotion turns into mindless superstition that Richler moves in satirically, as he did in *Son of a Smaller Hero* when he described the emotionalism evoked at Wolf Adler's funeral by the false report that he had died trying to save some scrolls of the Torah from burning, when in fact he was seeking for money which he mistakenly thought his father, tyrannical old Melech, had secreted in the same box.

The liberal or reform Jews, on the other hand, he regards as the true targets for satire. Their beliefs have lost conviction, and this makes it easy for them to make common ground with Christians whose faith has similarly lost its strength, so that they are willing to find a vaguely ethical middle ground with Jews or with anyone else who is willing to co-operate with them. A middle-of-the-road Judeo-Christian attitude appears, as bland and meaningless as Unitarianism and similar attempts to confuse religions and ethics. The sentimental desire to preserve the remnants of an ancient liturgy and yet remove all suggestions of superstition or social backwardness results in a middle class cult without real direction or meaning or anything but a code of behaviour observed on Sabbath only and a social focus within which the remaining rituals of the tribe, suitably sanitized, can be performed. It is this pretence of a religion — as it seems to him — that Richler satirizes in the scene of Bernie Cohen's *bar mitzvah* and in the showing of the film that Friar makes of it.

The politics that Richler deals with, at least in his earlier novels, is — as we have seen — local in the sense that he is concerned not with Canadian leaders and parties and their policies, but with the politics of St. Urbain Street, which tended to be extra-Canadian at the time of which Richler is writing — either Zionist or Communist. And among the Communists the objects of his satire are not so much the working class comrades like Panofsky of The Peoples Tobacco & Soda, or Panofsky's son Aaron who was crippled fighting in Spain. Rather he attacks the men of uncertain ethics like Uncle Benjy, who combine success in the capitalist world with a sentimental and con-science-solving dedication to its destruction. Marxism, with Uncle Benjy, becomes an intellectual toy, as Freudianism does with Aunt Ida, but here again Richler is intent on isolating the cult from the reality, on showing the difference between Marx and those who call themselves Marxists, between Freud and those who call themselves Freudians.

Wisely, perhaps because he recognized the real existence of Hugh MacLennan's "two solitudes," Richler refrains from satirizing the inhabitants and the institutions of French-speaking Montreal; when in the Québec countryside he concerns himself only with Jewish enclaves. But he does not leave untouched the WASP establishment that in the 1950s still insecurely ruled the city, whether he is consid-ering on the socially higher level, with the Westmount millionaire Calder and his rich bitch daughter, or on a lower level, with the absurd situation at Fletcher's Field School, where under the Protes-tant School Board a student body consisting almost entirely of Jewish children from Eastern European families is taught by a corps of WASP teachers, some at least of whom show strong signs of anti-Semitism. Richler's aim is not to attack the WASP teachers for being WASPs, but to show from the other side the absurdity of the divisions that can exist because of the prejudices that separate people who share the same land and the same city and must forge a life together within that environment. Jews and WASPs frozen into antagonistic positions are in his view equally absurd.

The satiric methods that Richler uses are mainly mockery, exaggeration, and the revelation of incongruity in action or attitude, and usually a combination of the three. An example is the description of the march of the High School Officers' Training Corps through the streets of the ghetto. The pompous antics of the WASP old army man who acts as commandant and the deficiencies of the performers in the band are exaggerated to the point of farce, and the mockery comes from the other characters, as smaller children jeer in the streets, and as one of the bandsmen is dragged out of the ranks by his grandfather to make up the number of men needed for prayers in a small synagogue. But underlying it all is the comic incongruity of these sons of East European immigrants whose families have no links or sympathies with Britain or its traditions playing at soldiers in the British manner. The ghosts of empire parade in strange disguise.

Again, when the film of the *bar mitzvah* is shown, there is the incongruity between the solemn and pseudo-anthropological script, calculated to suit the reform congregation, and the absurdities of some of the shots as seen through the eyes of the audience, whose joking commentary on the actions of people they know provides the mockery that brings down to earth the pretensions of the wretched film-maker and of the rabbi who figures so pompously in the ceremony and then at the end remarks: "A most edifying experience. . . . A work of art" (159).

But, of course, the major part of the satire is directed against Duddy himself, his pretensions, and the absurd actions into which he is forced in order to fulfil them. And perhaps it marks the degree of Richler's success in *The Apprenticeship* that while Duddy is the centre of mockery, on the part of the other characters and covertly of the readers as well, while everything he does is exaggerated to the point of farce by a kind of psychotic excitement, while at almost every critical moment in the novel we are aware of the incongruity between the lyrically expressed pastoral longings of old Simcha and the unscrupulous and often brutal methods his grandson uses to realize these longings, Duddy does not become a mere puppet of the satirical attitude like, say, the king of Brobdingnag in *Gulliver's Travels*, there merely to focus our discontent with the world as it is. He is still a human being with whom we can feel, even when we do not like him, and whose difficulties stir us even if we do not relish the means he used to overcome them. Perhaps this is because Richler makes us feel that while observing Duddy in action we are seeing the aspects of ourselves which we usually keep in control, and do not care to acknowledge, taking on flesh and running free. He walks — or rather runs — beside us like a mocking shadow. And to create for the reader such a credible double is surely the great achievement for a satirist, because he is then reaching out of his book and its special world and making his character and all he does a mirror for mankind.

IMAGINATIVE DARKNESS

As we have seen, critics like Leslie Fiedler long ago observed the darker side of Richler, "his lust for surreal exaggeration and the grotesque," and more recently, in accordance with current critical stances, others have noted a tendency in him towards deconstructionism, the breaking down of accepted standards of taste and hence of style, which of course is the opposite of the satirist's urge towards recreating order.

The interest in the horrific and the absurd, which becomes so much more evident in later novels like *Cocksure*, is of course in its way related to Richler's satiric bent, but there are times when it seems to go beyond the needs of satire as a critical and corrective discipline towards an almost nihilist breaking down of standards. As such it appears in Duddy's cynical exploitation of the unfortunate Virgil, first epileptic and then an irremediable cripple through Duddy's fault.

And yet Duddy is never the complete monster, like Richler's character Karp in *A Choice of Enemies* or the Star Maker in *Cocksure*. He has his extenuating circumstances — the difficulty of raising money to finance a quest that begins as an ideal — and he does have his moments of misgiving, in the cases of McPherson's wife and Virgil, and reacts with the violence of a guilty mind to Yvette's criticisms of his actions. Perhaps this was one of the reasons why Leslie Fiedler described *The Apprenticeship* as "a book which seems always on the verge of becoming truly obscene, but stops short, alas, at the merely funny" (Sheps 105).

Here Fiedler is hinting at a conservatism which balances the deconstructionist urge in Richler. It is the conservatism which goes naturally with the role of the satirist and with his desire to return men to the good ways of a pristine society; the conservatism that lurks beneath the surface in all the great satirists, whether we think of Swift or of Orwell or of Richler's Canadian predecessors, Haliburton and McCulloch. And it accords with Richler's own statement to Nathan Cohen that in his novels:

> I mean to say what I feel about values and about people living in a time when to my mind there is no agreement on values. (Sheps 29)

In other words, one way of interpreting *The Apprenticeship* is as a defence of a stable world of values against the leaching out of personal values that can be observed in almost every character in the novel, with the exception of the old orthodox Jews and the uninteresting Yvette. And it is this aspect of Richler that Fiedler denounces in another of his remarks delivered from an avant-gardist viewpoint:

> Satire was his special affinity — not, to be sure, polished and urbane satire, but shrill and joyously vulgar travesty — directed, all the same, against pop culture, on the one hand, and advanced experimental art on the other: middlebrow satire, in fact, however deliciously gross, an anti-genteel defence of the genteel tradition. (Sheps 103)

And yet, as in all of Richler's novels with the possible exception of his most autobiographical book, *Son of a Smaller Hero*, there is a dark side to Richler's imagination which does get out of control, a Satanic affinity that is exhibited in some of his more completely negative characters, like Kraus in *The Acrobats*, Karp in *A Choice of Enemies*, and, of course, the Boy Wonder in *The Apprenticeship*, who is so much more than a foe and a foil to Duddy.

The Boy Wonder is a figure who stands on the verge between the credible and the fantastic; he has not moved over entirely into the world of fantasy like the monstrous Star Maker in *Cocksure*. On his fantastic side he is a true Satan in miniature, a veritable fallen angel figure, struck down from handsomeness and promise at the age of twenty-eight by polio and turned into a physical grotesque with only the vestiges of his past beauty remaining.

At thirty he was no longer a handsome man. His shoulders and chest developed enormously and his legs dwindled to thin bony sticks. He put on lots of weight. Everywhere he went the Boy Wonder huffed and puffed and had to wipe the sweat from the back of his rolled hairy neck with a handkerchief. The bony head suddenly seemed massive. The grey inquisitor's eyes whether hidden behind dark glasses — an affectation he abhorred — or flashing under rimless ones unfailingly led people to look over his shoulder or down at the floor. His curly black hair had dried. The mouth began to turn down sharply at the corners. But the most noticeable and unexplained change was in the flesh of his face. After his illness it turned red and wet and shiny. His teeth, however, remained as white as ever and his smile was still unnervingly fresh.

The smile that somehow retained an aura of innocence made those who feared or disliked the Boy Wonder resent him all the more. (132–33)

The Boy Wonder is no mere brutal monster; in fact, he avoids getting involved in bloodshed. He reads seriously and is interested in the arts; he poses as a "God-fearing man" and he does not "smoke or drive his car or place bets on the Sabbath." He mocks the Jews of the reform temple and so identifies himself with the orthodox. Yet on every other day but the Sabbath he is running his night clubs and gambling halls, importing cocaine, and generally helping to keep Montreal a sinful city. And he remains throughout the novel the dark presence, indirect or direct, in Duddy's life.

Such figures as the Boy Wonder exist in Richler's novels as focuses of evil against whom it is hard for those who have no real values of their own to struggle. Kraus, the Nazi refugee in Franco's Spain, kills André in *The Acrobats*, and the Star Maker sets out to have Mortimer Griffin killed in *Cocksure*. The Boy Wonder does not destroy Duddy Kravitz in *The Apprenticeship*; indeed, in the last scenes he seems to be defeated by him. But in no sense are we led to feel that this is a triumph of good over evil, of honour over dishonour, of true values over false values. It is perhaps a temporary triumph of cunning over power, without moral reverberations. And in this sense, like Richler's other dark figures, the Boy Wonder is the destroyer, having called up from within Duddy the "regular behemoth" that Uncle Benjy had seen inside him. And so in *The Apprenticeship*, as in some of Richler's other novels, we see the forces of the imagination going their own dark way and effectively negating the novelist's rational intentions.

As a didactic novel, attempting to teach Richler's lessons of the need for values to re-emerge in a world that has lost them, *The Apprenticeship* may seem a failure. But as a work of the imagination, of realism and fantasy, painting a world in the bold dark and light chiaroscuro of human existence, and read for its own sake, without moralistic side thoughts, it is still perhaps Richler's most successful novel.

Works Cited

Bevan, A.R. Introduction. *The Apprenticeship of Duddy Kravitz*. By Mordecai Richler. New Canadian Library 66. Toronto: McClelland, 1969. n. pag.

Bevan sees the novel as a *Bildungsroman* in which the protagonist makes an affirmative choice at the end. In style and technique, Richler is a "traditionalist," but he handles dialogue very well.

Bowering, George. "And the Sun Goes Down: Richler's First Novel." *Canadian Literature* 29 (1966): 7–17.

Discusses the influence of Hemingway on Richler's style.

Brown, Russell. "Richler, Mordecai." *Oxford Companion to Canadian Literature*. Ed. William Toye. Toronto: Oxford UP, 1983.

Cameron, Donald. "Don Mordecai and the Hardhats." *Canadian Forum* March 1972: 29–33.

A straightforward and skilful skewering of Richler's anti-nationalist pieces.

_____ . "Mordecai Richler: The Reticent Moralist." *Conversations with Canadian Novelists*. 2 vols. Toronto: Macmillan, 1973. 2: 114–27.

Cohen, Nathan. "A Conversation with Mordecai Richler." *Tamarack Review* 2 (1957): 6–23.

Richler comments on his decision to leave Canada, his feelings about being an expatriate, his literary influences, the writing of *The Acrobats* and critical reception of his first two books, and his forays into journalism and scriptwriting.

Darling, Michael. "Mordecai Richler: An Annotated Bibliography." *The Annotated Bibliography of Canada's Major Authors*. Ed. Robert Lecker and Jack David. Vol. I. Downsview, ON: ECW, 1979. 155–211.

_____ , ed. *Perspectives on Mordecai Richler*. Toronto: ECW, 1986.

A collection of eight essays examining Richler's approach to history, his use of language, and his often misunderstood moral vision.

Davidson, Arnold E. *Mordecai Richler*. Literature and Life Series. New York: Unger, 1983.

Fiedler, Leslie. "Some Notes on the Jewish Novel in English." *Running Man* 1.2 (1968): 18–21.

Frye, Northrop. Conclusion. *Literary History of Canada: Canadian Literature in English.* Ed. Carl F. Klinck. 2nd ed. 3 vols. Toronto: U of Toronto P, 1976. 3: 318–32.

Gibson, Graeme. "Mordecai Richler." *Eleven Canadian Novelists.* Toronto: Anansi, 1973. 265–99.

Richler talks about writing, film, critics, and his novels.

Goodman, Walter. "Mordecai Richler Then and Now." *New York Times Book Review* 22 June 1980: 11, 22–24.

Kattan, Naïm. "Mordecai Richler: Craftsman or Artist." Trans. George Woodcock. *Canadian Literature* 21 (1964): 46–51.

Although he sees *The Apprenticeship of Duddy Kravitz* as the author's most accomplished work, Kattan condemns Richler for never having gone beyond his adolescence. Richler's characters are only uncomprehending caricatures and his world is "sentimental and false."

Knelman, Martin. "You See, Duddy, You See?" *This Is Where We Came In: The Career and Character of Canadian Film.* Toronto: McClelland, 1977. 99–114.

Concerns the making of the movie *The Apprenticeship of Duddy Kravitz.* Includes biographical details of Richler's life and critical reactions to his work.

Levine, Mark. *Mordecai Richler.* Profiles in Canadian Literature. Toronto: Dundurn, 1980.

McPherson, Hugo. "Fiction: 1940–1960." *Literary History of Canada: Canadian Literature in English.* Ed. Carl F. Klinck. 2nd ed. 3 vols. Toronto: U of Toronto P, 1976. 3: 205–33.

Compares Richler to the English "angry young men" and American "beat" writers in his attempts to expose pretentiousness.

Mathews, Robin. "Messiah or Judas: Mordecai Richler Comes Home." *Canadian Review* 1.1 (1974): 3–5.

McSweeney, Kerry. "Mordecai Richler." *Canadian Writers and Their Works.* Fiction Series, Vol. 6. Ed. Robert Lecker, Jack David, Ellen Quigley. Toronto: ECW, 1985. 129–79.

A critical examination of Richler's works, with additional sections on biography, tradition and milieu, and critical overview and context.

Metcalf, John. "Black Humour: An Interview with Mordecai Richler." *Journal of Canadian Fiction* 3.1 (1974): 73–76.

Moss, John. *Patterns of Isolation in English-Canadian Fiction.* Toronto: McClelland, 1974. 227–30.

_____ . *Sex and Violence in the Canadian Novel: The Ancestral Present.* Toronto: McClelland, 1977. 123–25, 131–39, 144–45.

_____ . "Mordecai Richler." *A Reader's Guide to the Canadian Novel.* Toronto: McClelland, 1981. 236–43.

Although Moss commends the satirical aspects of *The Apprenticeship of Duddy Kravitz,* as well as Richler's prose style and use of imagery, he thinks the novel lacks a certain "quality of heart." Moss concludes that "the whole novel is convincing, without being believable."

_____. "Richler's Horseman." *The Canadian Novel: Here and Now*. Ed. John Moss. Toronto: NC, 1978. 156–65.

New, William H. "The Apprenticeship of Discovery: Richler and MacLennan." *Canadian Literature* 29 (Summer 1966): 18–33.

In this comparison of *The Apprenticeship of Duddy Kravitz* and Hugh MacLennan's *The Watch That Ends the Night*, New concludes that Duddy and Jerome Martell are alike in the lack of close relationships with their parents, and in their search for selfhood.

Richler, Mordecai. *The Acrobats*. London: Deutsch, 1954.

_____. *Son of a Smaller Hero*. 1955. New Canadian Library 45. Toronto: McClelland, 1965.

_____. *A Choice of Enemies*. 1957. New Canadian Library 136. Toronto: McClelland, 1977.

_____. *The Apprenticeship of Duddy Kravitz*. 1959. New Canadian Library 66. Toronto: McClelland, 1969.

_____. *The Incomparable Atuk*. 1963. New Canadian Library 79. Toronto: McClelland, 1971.

_____. *Cocksure*. 1968. New Canadian Library 190. Toronto: McClelland, 1986.

_____. *Hunting Tigers under Glass: Essays and Reports*. Toronto: McClelland, 1968.

_____. *The Street*. Toronto: McClelland, 1969.

_____, ed. *Canadian Writing Today*. Harmondsworth: Penguin, 1970.

_____. *St. Urbain's Horseman*. 1972. New Canadian Library 185. Toronto: McClelland, 1985.

_____. *Shovelling Trouble*. Toronto: McClelland, 1972.

_____. *Notes on an Endangered Species and Others*. New York: Knopf, 1974.

_____. *Jacob Two-Two Meets the Hooded Fang*. Toronto: McClelland, 1975.

_____. *Images of Spain*. Photographs by Peter Christopher. Toronto: McClelland, 1977.

_____. *The Great Comic Book Heroes and Other Essays*. New Canadian Library 152. Toronto: McClelland, 1978.

_____. *Joshua Then and Now*. Toronto: McClelland, 1980.

_____. *Home Sweet Home: My Canadian Album*. Toronto: McClelland, 1984.

_____. *Solomon Gursky Was Here*. Toronto: Viking-Penguin, 1989.

Sheps, C. David, ed. *Mordecai Richler*. Critical Views on Canadian Writers 6. Toronto: McGraw-Hill Ryerson, 1971.

Tallman, Warren. "Need for Laughter." *Canadian Literature* 56 (1973): 71–83.

_____. "Wolf in the Snow." *A Choice of Critics: Selections from Canadian Literature*. Ed. George Woodcock. Toronto: Oxford UP, 1966. 53–76.

Duddy is different from other characters in the book in that he is not concerned with maintaining false appearances. Tallman sees Duddy's emotions as being real and sincere, unlike the others whose ideal — the Boy Wonder — suggests the limitations of their dreams.

Thomas, Clara. "Mordecai Richler." *Our Nature — Our Voices: A Guidebook to English Canadian Literature.* Toronto: new, 1972. 161–65.

    A survey of Richler's novels, emphasizing the themes of "Jewish experience, the writer-artist and Canadian society and its attitudes." Duddy is seen as Richler's most successful character.

Woodcock, George. *Mordecai Richler.* Canadian Writers 6. Toronto: McClelland, 1971.

    Discusses Richler's novels to *Cocksure. The Apprenticeship of Duddy Kravitz* is seen as Richler's best book, due to the convincing character of Duddy, "without rival Richler's most memorable creation."

———. "Richler, Mordecai." *Contemporary Novelists.* Ed. James Vinson. London: St. James, 1976. 1165–69.

Index